EL PASO LAWMAN

G.W.Campbell

by

Fred R. Egloff

Intoduction by C. L. Sonnichsen

THE EARLY WEST SERIES

CREATIVE PUBLISHING COMPANY
BOX 9292, PH. 713-846-7907
COLLEGE STATION, TEXAS 77840

El Paso Lawman
G. W. Campbell

Egloff, Fred R., 1954—
    El Paso lawman.

    (The Early West series)
    Bibliography:p.
    Includes index.
    1. Campbell, George W., 1850—1881. 2 Peace officers—Texas—
El Paso—Biography. 3. El Paso (Texas)—Biography. 4. Frontier and
pioneer life—Texas—El Paso. I. Title. II. Series.
F394.E4E37 1983   976.4'96 [B]   82—17169

    ISBN 0-932702-22-8, Reg. Edition, First Printing, 1982, 1500 copies
        ISBN 0-932702-24-4, Paperback Edition, 1982, 1500 copies
    ISBN 0-932702-23-6, Leatherbound Collector's Edition, 25 copies

DEDICATED TO
all my good friends
"out in the West Texas
town of El Paso"

Table of Contents

Dr. C. L. Sonnichsen is a noted historian on Western history, having spent his career as a professor of English and the literature of the Southwest. Since leaving academic circles, Dr. Sonnichsen has held several positions with the Arizona Historical Society, including that of Senior Editor of the Journal of Arizona History.

Introduction

The death of George W. Campbell, gunned down on the streets of El Paso, Texas, on April 14, 1881, and decried by popular historians as one of the bad guys in a famous shootout, reminds a thoughtful reader that Western America is often the victim of its own folklore. The mythical West—the West that Never Was—is as real to most Americans, and to many Europeans, as the true historical West, and it colors their judgment of men and events even in our skeptical, cynical, disillusioned generation. Since World War II our faith in the romanticized West has declined to the vanishing point, but the ideas implanted in our collective subconscious by hundreds of movies and popular novels during the first half of the century refuse to disappear. Jeni Calder sums up the situation in the title of her 1974 book: *There Must Be a Lone Ranger.*

The world of the traditional western—film or fiction—was simple and straightforward. The good men lined up on one side and the bad ones on the other. It was easy to tell them apart. *Time* magazine in a 1959 essay called, "The American

Morality Play," commented on "the visual language of the western:"

> The Good Guy wore a white hat, the Bad Guy a black
> hat. G.G. was clean-shaven. B.G. had five-o'clock shad-
> ow, and an experienced horse fan could predict the depth
> of the villain's depravity by the length of his sideburns.
> The villain chased the hero from right to left, but when
> the hero was winning, he was naturally headed right
> (with his pistol hand closest to the camera).

In those early days there was no middle ground between fictional virtue and vice. The hero, it is true, was often a "morally ambiguous character" (John C. Cawelti in *Focus on the Western)*, but he always changed the color of his hat in mid-story, as Destry did when he rode again in Max Brand's novel, and ended on the side of the angels. In a few cases, Jack Schaefer's *Shane*, for example, the angels seemed close at hand. A mysterious savior, transcending humanity, rode out of the everywhere into the here, righted great wrongs, and disappeared into the mysterious realm from whence he came.

Life, as we all know, is not that way. There are no angels among us and very few complete devils. Every man has redeeming features to balance his feet of clay, but the feet are always earthy, and much of our fiction is pessimistic about human nature. On the upper levels of the Western novel, as William P. Bloodworth points out (*Western American Literature*, Winter,

1980), "anti-heroes, non-heroes, or unsuccessful heroes" are the rule. Nevertheless we are still haunted by the need to see everyone in black and white. Stuart Lake made Wyatt Earp, a less-than-admirable frontier character, into a Galahad of Tombstone, and many—perhaps most—readers still believe that "Tombstone was lawless but one man was flawless." At the same time the McLaury brothers, Tom and Frank, who lost in the shootout near the O.K. Corral, were irrevocably branded as evil men. Vigorous protests have done no good. Ethel Robinson Macia, who lived through the violent times in Tombstone, used to tell how she tried in vain to persuade Walter Noble Burns that her friends Tom and Frank were not as he portrayed them. The latest attempt by McLaury supporters and relatives in Iowa to rescue the brothers from disgrace ("Were the McLaurys Peaceful Ranchers—or Gunslingers," Des Moines *Register*, November 1, 1981,) will probably have no effect either. The two men were scapegraces by popular demand. The Lone Ranger must have somebody to go up against.

It is obviously unfair to insist that every Westerner must appear in either a black hat or a white one. There should be a gray hat for men who are neither heroes nor villains. Wyatt Earp should certainly wear one. Another should be provided for George W. Campbell. Dallas Stoudenmire, the famous town-taming marshal, who has worn a white hat ever since the encounter which resulted in the deaths of "four men in five seconds," should have been crowned with black.

Campbell has been portrayed for a full century, in Fred Egloff's words, as "a big-mouthed troublemaker, a drunk a rustler, and an all-around bad hombre." Egloff is convinced that George has been badly abused by the myth makers, and on the basis of new evidence he makes an excellent defense of his position.

It may be that we need the good guys and the bad guys of the mythical West—the brief fifteen or twenty years which give us the only heroic age we Americans will ever have. When a good man like George Campbell is blackened by the romancers, however, some repair work is needed. For every Walter Noble Burns or Stuart Lake, a Fred Egloff should be required.

C. L. Sonnichsen
Tucson, Arizona

Preface

The Campbell story was originally prepared as a talk for the Chicago Corral of the Westerners. This expanded and documented version came into being because of the assistance and encouragement of many people. First, thanks go to Dr. C. L. Sonnichsen, who edited the first draft and whipped the footnotes into line. Equal credit should go to George V. Campbell, my friend and fellow townsman, for providing access to his family archives. These treasures, including a scrapbook, photos, and the letters of George W. Campbell, provided an insight into the true understanding of George Campbell's character, and a stimulus for further research.

At El Paso, Mrs. Paul Harvey, daughter of Zach White, uncovered new and vital information among her father's papers.

At Henrietta, Judge Frank Douthitt of the 97th Judicial District of Texas, located and researched the minutes of the Commissioners Court of Clay County in its earliest days.

I am deeply indebted to the staffs of the El Paso Public Library, the Texas State Library in Austin, the New Mexico State Library, and the New Mexico State Records and Archives Center at Santa Fe, the Barker Texas History Center of the University of Texas at Austin, the library of the University of

Texas at El Paso, the Chicago Public Library, and the Wilmette, Illinois, Public Library. These institutions provided cheerful and efficient service and made research a pleasure.

Among the individuals, scattered across the West from California to Texas, and from Texas to Illinois, who put a shoulder to the wheel were Leon C. Metz, Bob McNellis, Bud Newman, Robert N. Mullin, Philip J. Rasch, Fern Lyon, Bill O'Neal, William H. Gilson, Elizabeth Brownell, Stacy Osgood, Melodee Mann, James G. Schneider, Orlando Romero, Richard Salazar, Ed Bartholomew, Millard McKinney, and Katherine Dorman. My best thanks to all.

Fred R. Egloff
Wilmette, Illinois

George W. Campbell (1850–1881) as he appeared at the age of 27. This photograph was taken at Ironton, Ohio, in 1877 during one of his trips home. (Courtesy of George V. Campbell.)

1

The Early Years

At the busy intersection of South El Paso Street and West San Antonio Avenue in downtown El Paso, a bronze plaque affixed to the wall of the venerable Hotel Paso del Norte reads: FOUR MEN IN FIVE SECONDS.[1] Near this spot on April 14, 1881, four men were shot to death at almost the same instant, and newspapers in places as far away as Santa Fe, Kansas City, and Chicago hit the streets with headlines which screamed "Bloody Battle," and "War Raging in El Paso."[2]

The story has been told in many versions since. Feature writers, popular historians, and novelists have recounted—and embroidered—that brief and bloody chapter in the town's annals,[3] most of them presenting the encounter as the classic Western confrontation between good and evil; the good emerging triumphant. Marshal Dallas Stoudenmire has been hailed as the town-taming hero. The villain's role has been assigned to ex-marshal George W. Campbell, who had resigned his post some weeks before Stoudenmire's arrival. Campbell had feuded with the city fathers until a week before the advent of the railroad. He stopped one of Stoudenmire's bullets in a shoot-out and died the next day. Although some accounts credit Campbell with "a fair education and respectable family," he is usually pictured as a big-mouthed troublemaker, drunk, rustler, and an all-around bad hombre. According to the popular portrayals of the events of that tragic day, he deserved what he got.

There are good reasons, however, to believe that the popular portrayals are wrong and that Campbell has been unfairly condemned. Almost a hundred years after his death, and some 1500 miles away, the truth began to emerge as a result of a conversation with my friend and neighbor, George V. Campbell of Wilmette, Illinois. It was discovered that we shared an interest in Western history, and George revealed that his great uncle had once been the city marshal of El Paso, Texas. Could this relative have been George W. Campbell? The answer was yes. And that was not all. The family possessed letters, newspaper clippings, a scrapbook, and Campbell's six-shooter.

A study of these surviving remnants of history provided evidence that the real George W. Campbell was an entirely different person from the degenerate Kentuckian portrayed by popular historians and novelists—one of a breed of "shiftless, slovenly men without roots," as Matthew Braun's fiction describes them, "warped in mind and filthy by choice, willing to cut their own mother's throat for a decent meal, or a shot of cheap whiskey."[4] The letters and the family scrapbook presented a flesh-and-blood man, compassionate, deeply interested in his relatives and their children, disturbed by blood sport, and opposed to gambling. He was interested in the law and was versed in its intricacies. People of proven worth respected and praised him. Like all human beings, he had his faults, but his virtues far outweighed them.

George Campbell came of good pioneer stock, with roots in Colonial America; his ancestors came from Virginia and the Philadelphia area. One of his forebears served in the army of Great Britain under General Braddock in the war against the French and Indians.[5] Other forefathers fought for the American cause during the Revolution, participating in the southern campaign under General Greene at such battles as Guilford Courthouse and Eutaw Springs. Names in George's lineage include Mead, Keyser, Kelly, and Powell. He had reason to be proud of his heritage, and his own career, brief and tragic as it was, was creditable to him and to his ancestors.

George Washington Campbell, born on December 23, 1850, in Greenup County, Kentucky, was the youngest of the five children of George W. Campbell and Mary Ann Powell Campbell. He was named for his father, who died six months before his birth. His mother passed on when he was only nine years old, and the four boys and one girl were undoubtedly raised by one of their close relatives living in or near Ashland, Kentucky. His eldest brother William served in the Confederate Army, was captured, and died from wounds while in prison at Fort Delaware, Delaware, in 1865.[6]

George, too young for military service, felt the effects of the Civil War. The depressed conditions which gripped the country after the struggle ended caused many young men to leave home to try to make a place for themselves in the West. George headed for Texas. Perhaps he had been influenced by his cousin Lott Pratt Mead, a Confederate soldier who was stranded in

Texas at the conclusion of the war. Lott drove cattle for a time and eventually established a successful hundred-acre farm at Hill City, Texas, in 1872. George undoubtedly learned of opportunities in Texas from Lott when he returned to Kentucky to move his father and his family to his new home.[7]

George may have had personal reasons for wanting to get away since he seemed to have been in trouble because of a drinking problem. In one of his early letters, he notes that he had been abstaining, and he declared his intention not to return home until he had overcome his desire for stimulants. Since he returned several times to Kentucky, he may have solved his problem.

His earliest letter from Texas, written in the summer of 1875 to his sister Mary, placed him at Salt Creek, Montague County—a postoffice at a small settlement adjacent to Red River Station. The Chisholm Trail crossed the Red River on the border between Texas and the Indian Territory, at this point. Spanish Fort on modern maps is in the approximate area. George exhibited a sense of humor and seemed to be enjoying himself.

Salt Creek, Texas
Montague Co. June 21, 1875
Dear Sister Mary,

Your kind letter was handed me a few days ago and I was glad to hear from you. I received ones from Abe, Vince, and Mollie all the same day. One from Emma few days previous and also one from Charley Mead. I tell you it makes one blow just to answer them. I will answer Abe's through you, Vince's through Emma, so the number will be reduced to four. Now I can breathe easier.

In the first place Abe wanted to know what I was doing and how I was getting along. Well, poor e-nough, I suppose you will think, but it was a ground hog case with me. "Bound to have Meat." I am presently occupying the exalted position of *Chief Boss* of the culinary department at a cattle ranch. Wages are $20 a month and board. I expect to fill this position until the 1st of September. Then our cattle will be shipped to St. Louis and I *may* possibly get that far on my way home.

I tell you it is jolly to be cook. The boys will all have to mind me around camp. If they don't, I put a fly or bug in their coffee. We are living in fine style having killed a beef the day before yesterday. I have just gotten through *jerking* it. That is the Mexican style of drying. It is cut up in strips and hung in the sun for 2 or 3 days. It will never spoil. One of the owners of the ranch and his wife came up from headquarters a few days ago and stayed all night. They brought a wagon load of potatoes, new onions, beets, cucumbers and light bread. I nearly foundered myself eating. The Madame said to some of the boys that "George was a better cook than she could get." I wish you could stop in with Abe and the children some day and take dinner with us.

The broad canopy above us is our only shelter except some time when the rain wakes me up. I then crawl under the wagon. I got under one night when it was raining fearfully. It seemed as if the gates of heaven were let loose and just pouring the water out. The next morning when I awoke I was laying in water 4 inches deep. I did not experience a particle of inconvenience from being wet. I am getting fat and haven't shaved for 2 months. My whiskers are nearly an inch long, fully long enough for me.

I am sitting under the wagon (to keep from the sun) while writing this letter. I know if you had any idea how fatiguing it is you would say, "Well George I will let you off this time." Thus, I will take it for granted that you said so and quit. Tell Annie to write me a letter. I was sorry to hear of your sickness and Maimie's misfortune falling in the tub. You all must be careful and not let any accident happen to the little darling. I would love to see you all today. Whenever I get a letter from any of you I can hardly resist the temptation of starting for old Kentucky. Tell Annie to give my love to Miss B and that I'll be coming back to see her someday. . . . I received the Bible that Abe sent me. I also get a paper regularly. They are a treat to me, anything to read. Tell John G. that I have not touched a drop of whiskey since April and that I intend to stay here until I no longer have any desire to drink and dissipate. When I come home I want to find him a moral young man.

Well I might be as good as my word 2 pages back and quit. Much love to yourself and Abe and the children.

Your loving brother

Geo. C.

This early letter stands alone in the Campbell correspondence.[9] The next letter is dated five years later. Newspaper articles indicate, however, that George moved to the town of Henrietta in Clay County, Texas, in late 1875 or early 1876. The ranch for which he had been working may well have had its headquarters in the vicinity.[10]

NOTES

1. Harriet Howze Jones, *El Paso: A Centennial Portrait.* El Paso: El Paso County Historical Society, 1973, p. 286.

2. *Kansas City Evening Star,* April 15, 1881, *Chicago Tribune,* April 16, 1881, *The New Mexican* (Santa Fe), April 17, 1881: *Daily Interocean* (Chicago), April 17. 1881.

3. For example, James B. Gillett, *Six Years with the Texas Rangers.* New Haven: Yale University Press, 1925, pp. 232-235; Eugene Cunningham, *Triggernometry.* Caldwell, Ida.: Caxton Printers, 1941, pp. 171-178; Leon C. Metz, *Dallas Stoudenmire.* Austin: Pemberton Press, 1969, pp. 34-47.

4. Matthew Braun, *El Paso.* New York: Fawcett/Gold Medal, 1973, p. 46.

5. A. M. Pritchard, *Mead Relations.* Staunton, Va.: McClure & Co., 1933, p. 181.

6. W. W. Vann, letter to A. C. Campbell, Ashland, Ky. March 5, 1865 in possession of George V. Campbell, Wilmette, Illinois.

7. Pritchard, *Mead Relations*, p. 58.

8. Harry Sinclair Drago, *Red River Valley*. New York: Clarkson Potter, 1962, pp. 20-21.

9. Ranger Abstract Rolls, Archives, Texas State Library, Austin, Texas; Walter Prescott Webb, *The Texas Rangers: A Century of Frontier Defense*. Boston: Houghton Mifflin, 1935, p. 314; Leon C. Metz, *John Selman: Texas Gunfighter*. New York: Hastings House, pp. 75-82; C. L. Sonnichsen, *I'll Die Before I'll Run: The Story of the Great Feuds of Texas*. New York: Devin-Adair, 1962, pp. 159-162. G. W. Campbell, a Texas Ranger mentioned by Sonnichsen, was not the G. W. Campbell of this account.

10. *Henrietta Shield*, [April, 1881], undated clipping in possession of George V. Campbell.

Abram Croysdale Campbell, George's brother was the recipient of most of the letters written home by George. A. C. Campbell was an active developer of Ashland, Kentucky, where he was respected as a banker and builder. He owned the Ventura Hotel that he built in 1893. The former Campbell home still stands on the southwest corner of Bath Avenue and 13th Street and is part of the National Register. (Courtesy of George V. Campbell.)

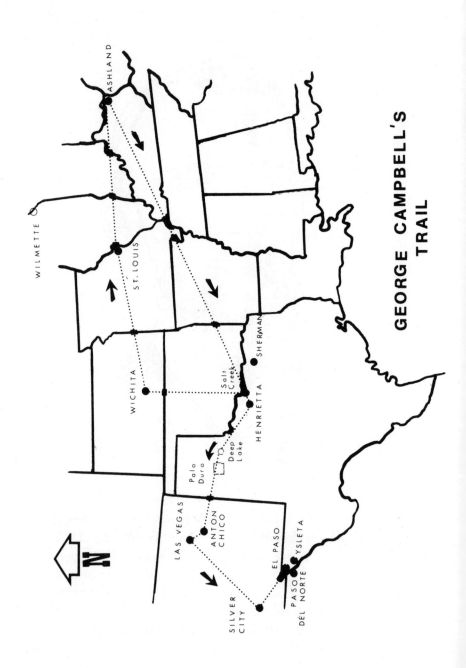

GEORGE CAMPBELL'S TRAIL

2

Texas Deputy Sheriff

The village of Henrietta, and Clay County as well, were organized in 1852. It was abandoned in 1862 because of Indian depredations and was not resettled and reorganized until 1873. Henrietta was indeed a frontier town in a transitional area and its culture was a unique blend of western and southern society.[1] George evidently fit in very well, for by the end of 1876 he had been appointed as deputy sheriff under John T. Craig.[2]

Clay County, during George's years of service, was the judicial center for the entire Texas Panhandle and for a number of other counties in its immediate area.[3] The enormous size of this territory can be appreciated when one realized that some locations in it were over 300 miles from the county seat; and since Clay County was located midway between the actively-used Chisholm and Western cattle trails, there were more desperadoes than other areas. George's job must have been demanding, but his second letter indicates that he had other things on his mind.

Office of John T. Craig   Henrietta, Texas

Sheriff, Clay County   October 26, 1879

Dear Bro. Abe,

Your letter came some days ago and I was truely glad to hear from all at home. I was quite sick at the time and word from home cheered me up. I am up again and feeling quiet well, but am not gaining strength very rapidly. Hope this will find all well at home.

Tell Mary and the children to write when they haven't anything else to do. Letters have been few and far between since my return. Tell Lillie she must grow and be a great big girl by the time Uncle George comes home again. Tell Maimie and Annie they must be good girls and go to school and learn to read and write, so they can write to Uncle George way off in Texas. I will have plenty to do all Fall and Winter and by Spring will be ready to return home again. One of our boys (Deputy ?) went home to Missouri a few weeks ago and returned last night with his wife. He done better than I did. I must say good bye for a while and I hope to hear from you soon. With love to all—and kisses for the children. (tell Mary she can have one too).

Your Bro.—Geo. W. Campbell

George's name turns up many times in the minutes of the Commissioners Court in connection with official business,[4] but almost nothing has been learned about his life and activities. No

Henrietta newspapers for the period are known to exist. The only ray of light comes from George himself and his correspondence.

Office of John T. Craig   Henrietta, Texas
Sheriff, Clay County   March 2nd, 1880

Dear Bro. Abe,

    I read your letter a few days ago and also the puzzle you sent. I have not had time to work on it yet. One party here claims he tried, but it cannot be solved. I will try as soon as I get more time. I am glad to hear that your business is booming. The Depot grounds will certainly enhance the value of your property. It would be a splendid place for a Hotel. I wish I were a hotel man and could take hold.

    There is a lot of talk here about the death of the City Marshal of Sherman. It was a sad affair. He was a very particular friend of mine, and was born and raird to manhood in Mason County, Kentucky. I was with him only a few days before he was killed. We were talking of the dangers in being an officer in Texas. He reminded me that here-to-fore I had been less careful in arresting criminals than I should be. He told me that his aim was never to let them get the drop on him. He returned to Sherman and the very next night was murdered in attempting to arrest a man. He killed one man and was in turn killed himself.

Texas has a fair showing for hanging. This spring some 12 or 15 are to be hung in April and May. 3 are to be hung in Cook Co., on the 30th of April. Rothschilds case was reversed and remanded for new trial. The Court below committed a grave error. One which any school boy who had ever been in Court, during a felony trial should have avoided. It was on that ground that our Court of appeals reversed the case. He permitted a jury-man who had formed and expressed an opinion to set as a juryman with that opinion still prevalent in his mind. He was certainly bought [sic] thinking by next trial the witness would be out of the way.

Hope this may find you all well. I am in splendid health.

Your Bro. Geo.

The marshal of Sherman, Texas, to whom George refers, was Sam Ball, who was shot in the chest as he was forcibly e-jecting Alf Johnson, a drunken troublemaker, from a bagnio. Ball seized his opponent's gun hand, drew his own pistol, and shot him dead. In turn, he was fired upon at close range and was blinded by Johnson's brothers, and died the next day from his wounds.[5]

The Rothschild trial was a famous case at Jefferson, Tex-as. Abe Rothschild's mistress, known as Diamond Bessie, was pregnant by him. He took her to Texas, where he proceeded first to marry and then murder her. At the end of trial, which spanned seven years, Abe was acquitted on a legal technicality.[6]

A clipping from the *Henrietta Shield* gives a general idea of George's record as a deputy sheriff; "George Campbell was one of the most efficient officers in position in this or any other county. He was brave as a lion, and as fearless as the Knights of olden times."[7] Judge W. B. Plemons echoed this opinion in a letter to Abe Campbell, "That boy was my friend, and no man ever had a truer or nobler hearted one. . . . I knew him well and intimately and during a period of his life that was calculated to show his traits of character, and to my mind no man with whom I was ever associated had a higher sense of honor or was his superior in all that it takes to constitute a true man."[8]

Plemons claimed to speak for the good citizens, the law-abiding men, of Clay County. He himself had a distinguished record in law enforcement, taking an active part in bringing the fence-cutting wars to a just and legal end.[9]

Wherever George was known, he earned good opinions. A Kentucky newspaper added its voice, "His honest, faithful and brave conduct in that office won for him a state reputation as an efficient and intrepid officer."[10] Years later Ranger Jim Gillett, who knew George well and was familiar with his reputation, wrote in his memoirs that as a Deputy Sheriff, Campbell "had done some good detective work. He was a good and efficient officer."[11]

Since George had achieved such a high standing in Clay County, the question arises: Why did he leave? The explanation probably lies in the political developments of West Texas. The

Panhandle and its many divisions were separated from the juris-
diction of Clay County in 1879. Shortly thereafter its other adjacent counties developed their own county courts. [12] This
shrinking of his realm probably contributed to George's deci-
sion to move west; no other reasons are known. He resigned his
position on May 15, 1880, and headed for New Mexico with seven companions. A letter written on June 8 provides a rare
glimpse of the terrain in very early days:

> We came west without anything to attract our at-
> tention, 180 miles, when we came to "Deep Lake."
> This is a lake of water in a very isolated part of the count-
> try. It is almost round, and about 75 yards in diameter—
> and the depth is not known—it is clear blue water very
> much like lake water of the North. There are no fish on
> it, but an abundance of "Water Dogs" and "Frogs." We
> came from Deep Lake to "Paladuro" Canyon 60 miles.
> "Paladuro is Spanish for "Hardwood." At the mouth of
> this Canyon is where the road goes up on the Plains—
> known as the Llano (Yanno) Estacado, or "Staked
> Plains." We travel from the point of starting up on the
> plains about 1 mile and reach an altitude from the start-
> ing point of about 350 feet. Then we are on the plains.
> To our left is "Paladuro" Canyon. This is an opening
> through the plains for 60 miles. At some points in this
> Canyon it is near 800 feet from the bottom to top or lev-
> el of plains. The Canyon is only about 1 mile wide at

first—but gradually widens out to 15 or 16 miles, enclos-
ing the most grand and imposing scenes as the eye of
Man ever beheld. There is certainly nothing in romantic
scenery to compare with it and yet it is comparatively unknown to the world. It is the hunting ground of the "Red
Man" the "pets of" our most glorious government. Bear,
black tail deer, cougar, and wolves abound in the Canyon
and are about the sole occupants. I had a curiosity to go
in the Canyon and fire off my gun. The reverbaration
lasted for several minutes. Echo, after echo repeating itself, making as some of the boys termed it—"Artificial
Thunder." At the 60 mile point we came to what is
termed the "door in the plains," being a narrow canyon on
the western slope of the plains. Before getting through
this canyon we were in New Mexico. The most barren
part of these U. S. it has ever been my fortune to behold.
How sheep and goats can live on the little grass they get
is a mystery to me. Yet they thrive and pay about 25%
on the investment. The secret of making this much profit
is the cheapness of labor.

Another letter reveals that the first New Mexican town he
entered was Anton Chico, a settlement on the Pecos River occu-
pied by 800 or 1000 inhabitants, mostly Mexican. "All Mexicans but 8 families," George reported, "and they are Germans. I
felt lost while there. Never hear the English language spoken,

only when I hunted up some dutchman to talk to. The Mexicans all say to me when spoken to 'No Suava.' "

At the end of a 500-mile journey the party came to Las Vegas, New Mexico, arriving on June 7, 1880. George found that he had gained thirteen pounds en route. Las Vegas was something of a metropolis in those days—a rail town on the Denver & Rio Grande with a population of 3000—and his arrival and departure went unnoticed by the *Optic*. The 1880 census was being taken there at that time, but he spent only a few days in town and was off again before the census taker got around to him. He had told his brother, "You can direct letters to me at Las Vegas care of the 1st National Bank,"[13] but he probably did not pick up many letters. Three months after his arrival he wrote:

> Las Vegas, N. M.
>
> August 27, 1880
>
> Dear Bro. Abe,
>
> Your letter arrived some days ago. I was away when it came. I have been on another long trip. On a hunt for stolen horses and cattle from Texas. Made a trip of 600 miles. I quit police business, did not like it. I am going to Silver City in a few days. May not return here, so don't write any more until you hear from me again. I send some views of Mexico and also a book. Hope this may find all well as I am. Will drop you a postal card now and then in my travels. Love to all
>
> Your Bro. Geo.

According to the *Ashland Independent*, back in the old home country, George was a marshal at Las Vegas,[14] but there is no record of his having held such an office. He was probably deputized or employed by a Texas cattle-raisers' association to go after cattle thieves. About this time, the Canadian River Association sent Frank Stewart and six men after a herd rustled by Billy the Kid's gang in the Texas Panhandle.[15] Early in November, 1880, Stewart met Pat Garrett at Las Vegas and several Panhandle cowboys assisted him in capturing the Kid. If George was with this group, he left it before the final act, headed for Silver City. The attraction was news of mineral strikes in that area. He established some claims, according to the *Independent*, but eventually ran out of funds and had to abandon them.[16]

NOTES

1. William C. Taylor, *A History of Clay County*. Austin, Texas: Jenkins, 1974, pp. 2-3, Katherine Douthitt, *Romance & Dim Trails*. Dallas: William Tardy 1938, pp. 1-4.

2. *Henrietta Shield*, [April, 1881]; *Ashland Independent*, [May, 1881], undated clipping in possession of George V. Campbell.

3. Taylor, *History of Clay County*, pp. 71-72; J. Evetts Haley, *Charles Goodnight*. Norman: University of Oklahoma Press, 1950, pp. 289-290.

4. Frank J. Douthitt, Judge, 97th Judicial District, Henrietta, Texas, to Fred R. Egloff, February 20, 1981.

5. *Chicago Tribune*, June 29, 1980.

6. Al Eason, "Queen of the West," *Old West*, Vol. 3, (Fall, 1967), p. 32.

7. *Henrietta Shield*, [April, 1881].

8. W. B. Plemons, letter to Abe Campbell, Henrietta, Texas, May 1, 1881.

9. William Buford Plemons served in the Confederate army, was wounded three times, was present at the surrender at Appomattox, served two terms as judge in Clay County, moved to Amarillo and was a judge in Potter County, later (1894) served in the Texas Legislature, was responsible for the "Four-Section Plan." See Taylor, *History of Clay County*, p. 93; Haley, *Charles Goodnight*, p. 401.

10. *Ashland Independent*, [May, 1881].

11. James B. Gillett, *Six Years with the Texas Rangers*. New Haven: Yale University Press, 1925, p. 233.

12. Taylor, *History of Clay County*, p. 72.

13. G. W. Campbell, letter to Abe Campbell, Las Vegas, New Mexico, June 8, 1880.

14. *Ashland Independent*, [May, 1881].

15. Charles A. Siringo, *A Texas Cowboy*. Lincoln: University of Nebraska Press, 1976, p. 125.

16. *Ashland Independent*, [May, 1881].

George Campbell may have been in a posse headed by Frank Stewart that was sent after a herd of cattle that had been rustled by Billy the Kid (shown here) and his gang in the fall of 1880.

William Buford Plemons was born in Macon County, Georgia, in 1844, served in the Confederate Army where he was wounded three times, and surrendered with Lee at Appomattox. Plemons settled at Henrietta, Texas, and later became mayor of that city. He served as judge of Clay County from 1876 to 1880 when he moved to Amarillo and became judge of Potter County. He was elected to the Texas Legislature in 1894. (Courtesy of the Panhandle-Plains Historical Museum, Canyon, TX.)

3
Turbulent El Paso

The next stop for George Campbell was El Paso. The Southern Pacific railroad, edging toward the border town where it was to meet other rail lines, was making the biggest news in that section of the country. Opportunity beckoned and many others besides George had responded. Here they felt they could get in on the ground floor of opportunity and build a prosperous future. Sometime during the month of November of 1880, George arrived in that dusty boom town, twenty-nine years old and anxious to make a place for himself. He was probably aware of the troubles brewing across the international border, but he most certainly knew nothing of the political undercurrents developing in the town itself. Had he known, he might have gone somewhere else and lived longer.

Situated on the Rio Grande opposite the older Mexican city of Paso del Norte (present-day Juarez), El Paso was incorporated in 1873. Three years later the city council was disbanded since no one was interested in keeping it alive. A violent confrontation took place in 1877 in the valley below El Paso at San Elizario when American opportunists attempted to set aside a tradition, which Mexicans on both sides of the river assumed to be a right: which had allowed the gathering of salt at a *salina* a hundred miles to the east. The Salt War left a legacy of smoldering resentment on both sides, caused the death of several Americans, and disgraced a unit of the Texas Rangers.[1] Other causes of bad feeling arose as time went on. In 1880, for example, a Ranger detachment was permitted to cross the border in pursuit of Victorio and his band, but when the Apaches were cornered, the Mexican commander ordered the Americans back to the United States to keep them from sharing the final victory with the Mexican Army.[2]

Whatever they may have felt about their neighbors across the river, border Americans kept their sentiments mostly to themselves. The population of El Paso before the arrival of the railroad was under 500, and Mexicans far outnumbered the Anglos. The impending arrival of the railroad sparked a boom, and an increasing number of Americans began to come to El Paso. By mid-1880 the population had grown to 700, and in the course of the following year it doubled.[3] A city government began to be urgently needed, and in July of 1880, merchant Solomon Schutz took charge as mayor. Later in the same month John B. Tays, commander of the Ranger unit at San Elizario during the Salt War, was appointed city marshal. He received no salary and was expected to live off his share of fines accessed against offenders whom he arrested. There was trouble almost immediately. Along with his peace-keeping function, Tays was charged with the additional duty of street maintenance, and a dispute arose when he repaired a large hole in one of the streets by filling it with refuse. He was removed from duty within three months of his appointment.[4]

A. I. Stevens succeeded him as marshal. He lasted a month and was removed for "neglect and dereliction of duty."[5] On December 1, 1880, George Campbell pinned on the marshal's badge after being recommended by Captain George Baylor, commander of the Ranger company stationed at Ysleta, county seat and largest valley town.[6] He was the third marshal of El Paso to be employed in a little over four months. He inherited an assistant marshal named Bill Johnson who had a badly-crippled arm, and was known as the town drunk. His father was a respected citizen, but Bill was not highly regarded.[7]

Most of El Paso's problems in the law-and-order department can be laid on the doorstep of Mayor Schutz, a prosperous merchant with stores on both sides of the river who used his considerable powers of persuasion to advance his own interests. In truth, he was somewhat of a con artist. The proof can be found in letters written home to Germany by young Ernst Kohlberg, who reveals that Solomon Schutz came to El Paso from Westphalia at the expense of his uncles, Samuel and Joseph Schutz; immediately fell out with them; opened his own store; and tried constantly to destroy their business. "One cannot imagine a greater hate than that they hold for each other," Kohlberg wrote. "This bitter feeling disturbs social intercourse in such a small community and makes it harder to live here."[8]

During a trip back to Germany, Solomon induced Ernst Kohlberg's parents to sign a contract with him. He agreed to provide transportation to El Paso for the lad, who would work for him. As a result, Ernst Kohlberg became virtually an indentured servant to Solomon Schutz. The boy protested in his letters home, "I do not feel that I have been justly treated," and he gave ample evidence that Schutz was taking advantage of him.[9]

The mayor was evidently using a similar technique on his city marshals. He would paint a glowing picture of the position and the opportunities it offered, but he would not provide pay. When Campbell was hired, he had been led to believe, as his hometown paper reported, that "he had a contract to receive money from fines; and that the council was to provide him with a reasonable allowance in addition to this, so as to make it a good salary. Not knowing what the fines would amount to, this extra amount was not fixed."[10]

George entered into his new duties with energy and optimism. He was handicapped by a lack of fluency in Spanish and his only assistant was unreliable, but he gave his best to the job until he ran head-on into Mayor Solomon Schutz. As the *Ashland Independent* told the story, "He made many arrests, and always without harshness or use of any arms. The Mayor, however, being a merchant made his office subservient to his business and either would not fine a Mexican, or make the fine very light because he was courting their trade, and so likewise with the Americans." [11]

Some of the blame for what happened, it must be admitted, was placed on Campbell's shoulders by his contemporaries. William Coldwell, attorney and later city recorder, was one of Campbell's critics. Years later he wrote that Campbell, under happier circumstances might have become a valuable citizen. He was "by no means vicious or naturally lawless. . . . was too unsophisticated and too upright to levy blackmail, and his connection with the disturbers of the public order was too intimate to make it a pleasant duty for him to be energetic in their arrest, conviction, and suppression."[12] The implication here is that the city fathers expected him to supplement his income by shaking down the gamblers and prostitutes.

Ranger Jim Gillett in his book, *Six Years with the Texas Rangers*, is another who questioned Campbell's friendships. "During this period, Campbell was very friendly with the sporting element in El Paso, especially the Manning brothers, who were running two saloons and a big variety theater."[13]

In the interest of accuracy it should be noted that although some of the Mannings were in El Paso when George arrived, Frank and Jim were running a ranch north of town at the time. Their first saloon was not opened until several months after his resignation.[14] Their variety theatre opened for business seven months after his death.[15] "Doc" Manning, who headed the clan, had not even arrived at the time of George's demise. It is hard to believe that an alliance could have developed so rapidly or that he could have abandoned his ideals as a responsible peace officer overnight. His friendship with Jim and Frank Manning probably matured after his brief tenure as city marshal. After all, he was indebted to the local Ranger commander for his job. Gillett, it should be added, was writing forty years after the event, and he exhibited a tendency to confuse the chronology of his own activities.

Seargent James B. Gillett of the Texas Rangers as he appeared in his later years. He became city marshal of El Paso, Texas, for a time. (Courtesy of Rose Collection.)

Ranger Frank Beaumont was probably closer to the truth in recounting his own version of the situation many years later when he was an officer of the Texas Ranger Association. He had served on the El Paso Ranger detail and was closer than Gillett to the actual events. "About this time, the town began to fill up with adventurers from all parts of the country," he said. "To keep things orderly the police force consisted of Marshal George Campbell, and an assistant. No braver man than Campbell ever carried a gun, but it was impossible for two men to hold down a place like El Paso was fast becoming. Campbell started a campaign of education among the inmates of several noted resorts and gave them a resaonable time to men their ways. The marshal's warning for a short time seemed to be taken in good part by the toughs." [16]

This shape-up-or-ship-out sort of approach to law enforcement must have been misconstrued as friendship with the bad element. His policy certainly did not add to his revenue but it made sense, considering how shorthanded he was and how serious his problems were.

As the end of the year approached, George wrote a brief letter to his brother revealing his state of mind at this crucial time in his life.

El Paso, Texas
December 20, 1880

Dear Bro. Abe,

Your letter and photograph to hand some days ago. Glad to hear you had a pleasant trip through the

El Paso. Tex
Dec 20th 1880

Dear Bro. Abe.

Your letter and
Photo. to hand some
days ago - glad to
hear you had a pleas-
ant trip through the
Mountains - I am
now City Marshal
here - Think I will
do well - I have better
health here than at any
place I have ever
been at - People coming
here from all parts of
the globe - Hope this
will find all well -
wish I could be with
you Christmas

no talk here about such a day coming about think I will get to "eat Yurkey". The Mexicans have been having their "annual feast" as they term it — which consists of ~~Bu~~ Bull fights — or rather fights between man and Bull — and all kinds of Gambling devices — I took the part in one day, but was disgusted with their brutality, and did not go any more — with love to all. and a merry happy Christmas!

Your Bro
George.

Mountains, I am now City Marshal here. Think I will do well. I have better health here then at any place I have ever been at. People coming here from all parts of the globe. Hope this will find all well. Wish I could be with you Christmas. No talk here about such a day coming—don't think I will get to "eat Turkey." The Mexicans have been having their annual feast, as they term it. Which consists of Bull fights—or rather fights between Man and Bull, plus all kinds of gambling devices. I took the feast in one day but was disgusted with their brutality and did not go any more. With love to all and a Merry happy Christmas.

Your Bro.

George

The "feast," of course, was the fiesta of Our Lady of Guadalupe, celebrated in Mexico on December 12. This festival continued for a couple of weeks. The optimistic tone of the letter indicates that the marshal did not yet know that additional compensation for his work would not be forthcoming. Three days later, on George's thirtieth birthday, he attended a meeting of the city council in the course of which the members agreed to send the following message to Governor O. M. Roberts:

Sir: Dec. 23, 1880

We the Mayor and Board of Aldermen of the City of El Paso, having under consideration the ways and means. . .

to better administer the law and city ordinance, to preserve order, and to protect life and property within the city limits. . . believe that the time has now come when. . we are unable to protect life and property. And the reasoning for such inability we respectfully assign the following:

1st. That the sheriff of this county and his deputies. . . reside fifteen miles distant.

2nd. A Marshal and Assistant Marshal, together with one Constable, constitute the police force of this city. The force is not stronger for want of funds. . . to provide compensation for police officers and to maintain the municipal government.

3rd. The Southern Pacific and the Rio Grande and El Paso Railways are on the eve of completion to this point. As the forerunners and followers of such enterprises, we now have turned loose upon us hordes of vagabonds, gamblers, burglars, thieves, and particularly murderers.

4th. Like classes have also poured into El Paso, Mexico one mile distant. . . and thus one place is a refuge for criminals and fugitives of the other. We have no doubt that in each of the El Pasos, confederates for crime are now being formed, with aids and confederates in the other. Therefore to the end that law may be enforced, peace and good order be preserved, and life and property be protected, we respectfully request that Colonel G. W. Baylor and his detachment of State forces now stationed at Ysleta, be ordered here for the purpose of aiding the municipal authority until such time as the municipality shall be able. . . to execute the law and its ordinances.[17]

This document is notable for what it says, and even for what it does not say. It admits to the understaffing of the local force and it uses as an excuse the lack of money—a specious subterfuge since the city had been issuing numerous licenses.[18] By implication George Campbell's record as a peace officer is approved—at least no negative view appears. The conclusion is inescapable that the letter is an attempt to secure protection at no expense to the city.

No record exists of a possible interchange between the marshal and his employers, but since the end of the month was approaching and food and lodging cost money, there is every reason to assume that George mentioned the acceleration of the boom, the consequent increase in his work load, and his need for compensation. There is no reason to doubt, either, that he got very little satisfaction from the council and had to be satisfied with the promise that assistance would be sought from the state. His thirtieth birthday closed on a very sour note.

NOTES

1.   C. L. Sonnichsen, *The El Paso Salt War*. El Paso: TWC Press, 1961.

2.   Webb, *The Texas Rangers*, p. 402; Gillett, *Six Years with the Texas Rangers*, p. 186.

3. *El Paso Daily Times*, January, 1882; Cleofas Calleros, *El Paso Then and Now*. El Paso: American Printing Company, 1954, p. 27.

4. C. L. Sonnichsen, *Pass of the North: Four Centuries on the Rio Grande*, El Paso: Texas Western Press, 1980, Vol. I, pp. 216-217; El Paso City Council Minutes, Book 2, p. 22.

5. Metz, *Dallas Stoudenmire*, p. 3; El Paso City Council Minutes, Book B, p. 37.

6. Captain George W. Baylor, letter to General W. H. King, September 30, 1881, Adjutant General's Office records, Barker History Center, University of Texas, Austin.

7. Gillett, *Six Years with the Texas Rangers*, p. 233; George Look, "Reminiscences," June 13, 1909," Ms., El Paso Public Library. Look arrived in the winter of 1880-81, traveling with the general manager of Adams Express. He boarded at Doyle's saloon in 1881 and claimed to have been an eyewitness to most of the major events of that time. He left town shortly after the gunfight of April 14, 1881, when someone shot at him one morning when he was at breakfast. When he returned, he became part owner of the Gem saloon and was said to have been involved in many shady transactions through the years. The influence of the father may explain how Bill Johnson was able to maintain a position for which he was so obviously un-suited. Look was evidently unfriendly to Campbell.

8. Ernst Kohlberg, *Letters of Ernst Kohlberg*, trans. Walter L. Kohlberg, ed. Eugene O. Porter. El Paso: TWC Press, 1973, p. 37.

9. Kohlberg, *Letters of Ernst Kohlberg*, pp. 5, 33-42.

10. *Ashland Independent*, [May, 1881].

11. *Ashland Independent*, [May, 1881].

12. W. M. Coldwell, review of Gillett's *Six Years with the Texas Rangers*, undated clipping from an El Paso newspaper, probably 1921, El Paso Public Library.

13. Gillett, *Six Years with the Texas Rangers*, p. 233.

14. *El Paso Times*, April 2, 1881. The first Manning saloon belonged to Frank and was located five miles west of El Paso near the end of the Southern Pacific tracks, then being laid into the city. Later he leased the old Ben Dowell saloon, where Hotel Paso del Norte was built in 1912. Jim and a partner entered the saloon business in April, at the Gem.

15. Metz, *Dallas Stoudenmire*, p. 97. The Variety Theatre opened on November 25, 1881.

16. *El Paso Herald*, November 13, 1909 (Beaumont's recollections).

17. El Paso City Council Minutes, Book B, p. 56.

18. Metz, *Dallas Stoudenmire*, p. 97; El Paso City Council Minutes, Book B, pp. 68-71.

*Solomon Schutz, Mayor of El Paso, in 1880. (Courtesy of
the Aultman Collection, El Paso Public Library.)*

Goerge W. Campbell on the left and Jim Manning, right, as they appeared in 1881. (Courtesy of George V. Campbell.)

4

El Paso Marshal

The final week in December of 1880 was as trying as its predecessors. More people descended on the city every day—a mixture of good and evil. A particularly ominous arrival stepped from the Mesilla stagecoach before the week was over. His name was Samuel M. (Doc) Cummings and he would soon open the Globe Restaurant while developing an active interest in local politics. According to James H. White, prominent El Pasoan and a later sheriff, Cummings had a reputation as a very dangerous individual in San Marcial, New Mexico. He proved to be a key figure in the drama which was building up toward a climax.[1]

Meanwhile the governor had responded to the council's plea for help by ordering Captain Baylor to move his force to El Paso, whose lodging was to be furnished by the city. It turned out that the city was unable or unwilling to provide quarters at boomtown prices, and early in January, 1881, the Rangers moved to rent-free accommodations at the Marsh Ranch four miles below town.

Their assignment was to assist Marshal Campbell in keeping order, but by the time they were ready to function, George was out of office. When the end of December arrived, he found that he was not going to get the allowance he had been expecting. Frustrated, he told Mayor Schutz what he could do with his

Captain George W. Baylor who was in charge of the Texas Rangers in the El Paso area recommended George Campbell for the office of city marshal. (Courtesy of the Western History Collection, University of Oklahoma.)

job and proceeded to sue the city for back pay. Captain Baylor noted later that Campbell won his case, but no record exists to show that he ever received compensation.[2]

During the next two weeks a rapid and confusing series of events took place. The parts of the jigsaw puzzle seem to fit together in the following order. The impending resignation of the marshal set the town up for what was probably the wildest New Year ever recorded in any town in the Old West. Word leaked out, or was intentionally passed around, that there would be no law enforcement on January 1, 1881. Campbell could hardly have been expected to conceal his rage, but there is no evidence that he encouraged the lawless element to take charge. Nonetheless, within an hour or two into 1881, all hell broke loose in El Paso. The downtown section was lit up with gun flashes. Ranger Gillett reports in one place that "some 50 or 100 shots" were discharged; in another he says that "some three or four hundred shots" were fired "promiscuously and with no attempt to make arrests."[3]

Captain George W. Baylor, Gillett's father-in-law, noted that "they paid marked attention in their pistol practice to his Honor the Mayor's store and private residence," but there were other targets that night. According to William Coldwell, the house of Alderman Adolf Krakauer was a focal point of attack. His door was knocked off its hinges by the impact of the bullets. How long and how extensive the lawless activity continued that night can only be conjectured. Newspapers in other cities did not report it—probably because it occurred on New Year's Eve.

George Campbell's part in the rioting, if any, has not been documented.[4] The fact that the mayor and a council member were attacked casts suspicion on him, but he was not the only one in town who despised the mayor. He can certainly be faulted for not maintaining order since his resignation had not been officially accepted.

When the sun rose on the bullet-scarred city, Mayor Schutz hastened to send a call for help to Captain Baylor. The call was answered very shortly by a squad of Rangers under Corporal Fitch.[5] Among the men who took up temporary quarters in the city was Frank Beaumont, whose report casts considerable light on what followed. He makes it clear that George had been embarrassed by the riot. Shortly after the Rangers arrived, George sought their help in running a gang of troublemakers out of town—apparently the same gang he had warned earlier.

One morning Campbell came to the rangers' quarters in the Overland building and said, "Boys, I think we have given these people time enough to make good. They are meaner than ever and I think the only way is to run them out of town. What do you think about it?" It did not take long for the rest of the boys to say that they agreed with him. Lum Teverly [Chris Peveler?] said, "George, it's a good idea. Let us start them on the run at once." After breakfast we called on them [the gang that made their headquarters at a place on the corner of El Paso and

San Antonio streets]. We asked them to call the three men who were making the most trouble. One of the men was inclined to be impudent, and he said he would call them when he got good and ready. A few words from the marshal made him see things in a different light. To end the matter we went through the house and soon found the men we were after. We told them we had given them fair warning and they must leave town inside of twenty-four hours. One said that a tenth of that time would do him. They crossed the river that same evening and made a new home in Paso del Norte.[6]

The conflict between Campbell and Mayor Schutz reached a new high a day or so later. George evidently thought of a way to bolster his sagging finances before his lawsuit was adjudicated. John W. Hampton reported, "He went into the Mayor's office to get a warrant for the purpose of arresting a party for whom he knew there had been a reward offered. The Mayor refused to issue the warrant, ordered Campbell out of his office, which caused an argument between them. The Mayor threatened to get his gun and shoot Campbell, and started into an adjoining room. Then Campbell stepped out onto the pavement, drew his revolver and challenged his foe to come out. The mayor did not accept his challenge. After Campbell had given his opinion of the mayor, he left. The mayor then issued a warrant for George, charging him with assault with intent to kill."[7]

It was evidently at the conclusion of this altercation that Campbell "rode through town in a hack, fired off his pistol and threatened to kill the mayor," as Captain Baylor wrote later.[8]

Mayor Schutz gave his warrant for serving to Assistant Marshal Johnson, who promptly sought Campbell out. George took the warrant, scribbled an obscenity on it, and told Bill to give it back to the mayor.[9] Schutz then sent the warrant, obscenity and all, to Captain Baylor at the Ranger headquarters. Baylor was incensed. Rangers Johnson and Weldon who were in El Paso to keep the peace, had been at the scene and had done nothing. Baylor wanted to know why and called the men in. They explained that Campbell "was a personal friend and they thought he was in the right, and they did not want to arrest him." Baylor promptly discharged both of them. "They would not do for Rangers," he said, "and they should arrest a brother if a warrant was put in their hands for him." He then sent Sergeant James B. Gillett and Corporal George Lloyd with the warrant to make the arrest. They were unable to locate George, and Baylor assumed that "he had skipped and gone to Johnny Hale's Ranch."[10]

John W. Hale and his ranch played an important part in Campbell's fate, though only a few scattered facts about the man and his place have ever been assembled. He had been born in 1845 in Iowa of English parents and the family had moved to California not long after his birth.[11] When President Lincoln called for troops from California during the Civil War, Hale was one of the first to sign up after the second call. He was no more

The John W. Hale family with Mrs. Hale seated at the left. Although there is no known photograph of John W. Hale, he has been described as being tall, over six feet in height. (Courtesy of the University of Oklahoma Press and Leon Metz.)

than sixteen or seventeen when he enlisted at Yreka, California, on September 12, 1861. He served as a private in Company A of the Fifth Regiment of Infantry, a unit which became part of Carleton's California Column, and marched across southern Arizona in 1862. Seeing no action other than some Indian skirmishes, the unit was stationed at several New Mexican posts, including Fort Fillmore. Hale was mustered out at Mesilla, New Mexico, on November 20, 1864, upon completion of his enlistment. Two months later he again enlisted. This time he served with Company E of the First Battalion of Veteran Infantry. Most of this tour was spent at Fort Craig, New Mexico. When he was mustered out two years later at Los Pinos (south of Albuquerque), his record for both tours was unblemished.[12] He was soon back in El Paso, and in 1870 he served in a posse charged with apprehending Frank Williams, who had taken a shot at Albert Fountain. Williams had killed Judge Gaylord Judd Clark before he could be subdued.[13] There were other creditable episodes in his record. Republican wheelhorse W. W. Mills related how Hale had befriended him in 1871 when his life was endangered at a gathering in San Elizario, providing him with arms after securing a pledge that they would not be used unless Mills was attacked.[14] When El Paso was first incorporated in 1873, Hale served for a very short time under Mayor Ben Dowell as the city's first marshal.[15] He lived with his wife Angelita on an eighty-acre ranch at Canutillo fourteen miles north of town. They had six children—one boy and five girls.[16] In 1880, the Manning brothers purchased an adjacent ranch and hired Hale as foreman.

Colonel Albert Jennings Fountain was a special United States district attorney in New Mexico and a powerful political leader of that state. John Hale was in the posse that apprehended Frank Williams for shooting at Fountain. Fountain mysteriously disappeared with his eight-year-old son in January 1896 while riding home in his wagon from Lincoln, and foul play has been suspected since, but not proven.

Canutillo, originally a Spanish land grant, was located in a *bosque* (thicket) where it could, and probably did, provide a refuge for smugglers and fugitives. In 1874 it was divided by court among Joseph Magoffin, Anson and W. W. Mills, and three others. They in turn disposed of subdivisions of their acreage, and Hale was among the purchasers.[17] Almost at once suspicion pointed to his place as a center of outlaw activity. It was at the western end of a smugglers' trail across the Franklin Mountains (the present-day Transmountain Highway follows this trail). The Mexican border was within easy reach. Hale's place was almost ideally situated to serve as an outlaw headquarters.

Captain Baylor was convinced that it was indeed an outlaw headquarters.[18] He recalled long afterward that he was scouting there in the winter when the leaves had fallen and noted that there were platforms in some of the big cottonwoods "where a thief could take a comfortable snooze up in a tree, whilst the rangers were looking for his trail on the ground.[19] One is left to wonder by whom and for whom these structures were built and where the fugitives would have hidden their horses.

When a Ranger was dismissed from active service, Baylor expected him to usually head for Hale's ranch, and it would have been the logical place for Campbell to seek refuge. He knew that a warrant was out for him, and he was undoubtedly short of cash. It should be noted, however, that according to John W. Hampton, Campbell did not run and hide. He was arrested by the Rangers and put under bond to appear for trial.[20]

It is possible that both Baylor and Hampton were telling the truth. George may have presented himself for arrest after securing bond money. Funds for the bond could have come from Hale's employers, the Mannings. At any rate, by January 14, 1881, the charges had been dropped and his resignation was accepted by the city council.[21] In the absence of records, one is obliged to resort to conjecture, but it is at least a strong possibility that there was some sort of plea bargaining related to the judgement awarded him in his suit for back pay.

On that very day, Ed Copeland was sworn in as the new marshal, and his salary was set at $50 a month. This indicates that the city could afford to pay a marshal, and that someone friendly with the saloon owners (as Campbell's detractors said he had been), was not objectionable to the council. Marshal Copeland owned and operated the Occidental Saloon. One month later, however, he was dismissed for not posting a $500 surety bond leaving only one person who wanted the marshal's job—Bill Johnson, the alcoholic deputy. He was sworn in as the fifth marshal in seven months. [22]

There is no record of George's residence or occupation at that time, but it is possible that he went to work for the Mannings. They evidently understood his plight and were sympathetic to him. Proof of their friendship may well exist in one of the two photos of George that have recently come to light. George is shown standing, holding a revolver. Seated next to him is an unidentified man wearing a Mexican sombrero who bears a striking resemblance to Jim Manning as he appears in contemporary photographs.

Association with the Manning brothers was not neces-
sarily a bad thing. They were probably not the hard cases that
popular historians make them out to be. Dr. C. L. Sonnichsen
notes that the Mannings had staunch defenders and adds, "The
feeling comes through in these evaluations that the Mannings
were peaceful and amiable until they felt put upon. Then somebody got hurt."[23] The fact that both George and the Mannings
were on the side of the South may have strengthened their
friendship. A member of Campbell's family had given his life for
the cause, and the brothers, according to Doc Manning's widow,
had an above-normal and lifelong dedication to the Confeder-
acy. There is the possibility that they may have met before the
El Paso days. Jim, Frank and John Manning drove cattle between East Texas and Kansas at the time George was a deputy
sheriff in Henrietta. William Manning was murdered in the
course of one drive and his brothers tracked down and killed his
slayer. There is no significant evidence of a previous association.[24]

NOTES

1. *El Paso Times*, April 2, 1881; Metz, *Dallas Stoudenmire*, p. 84, quoting James H. White.

2. Captain George W. Baylor, letter to General W. H.
King, September 30, 1881, Adjutant General's Office records.

3. Gillett, *Six Years with the Texas Rangers*, p. 233;
Frontier Times, July, 1924, p. 24.

4.   Captain George W. Baylor to General W. H. King, September 30, 1881, Adjutant General's Office records; Conrey Bryson, *The Land Where We Live*, El Paso: Guyness, 1973, pp. 40-41; L. C. Metz, *The Shooters*. El Paso, Mangan Books, 1976, p. 94.

5. *Frontier Times*, July, 1924, p. 24.

6. *El Paso Herald*, November 13, 1909.

7. *Ashland Independent*, [May, 1881].

8. Captain G. W. Baylor, letter to General W. H. King, September 30, 1881, Adjutant General's Office papers, Barker History Center, Austin.

9. Look, "Reminiscences," June 13, 1909, El Paso Public Library, Austin.

10. Captain G. W. Baylor, letter to General W. H. King, September 30, 1881, Adjutant General's Office papers, Barker History Center, Austin.

11. Metz, *Dallas Stoudenmire*, pp. 37-38.

12. Orton, Brig. Gen. R. H., *Record of California Men in the War of the Rebellion*, California, 1890; pp. 383-384, 406, 658, 673, 679.

13. Mills, W. W., *Forty Years at El Paso*, Chicago; W. B. Conkey, 1901, p. 148.

14. Mills, *Forty Years at El Paso*, p. 143.

15. White, Owen P., *Out of the Desert: The Historical Romance of El Paso*. El Paso: The McMath Co., 1924, n. 155; *El Paso Daily Times*, June 25, 1916.

16. Metz, *Dallas Stoudenmire*, pp. 37-38, 47.

17. Webb, W. P., *Handbook of Texas*, Vol. 1, p. 291.

18. Captain G. W. Baylor to General W. H. King, September 30, 1881, Adjutant General's Office Papers, Barker History Center, Austin.

19. *El Paso Herald*, January 10, 1906.

20. *Ashland Independent*, [May, 1881].

21. Metz, *Dallas Stoudenmire*, p. 8.

22. Metz, *Dallas Stoudenmire*, p. 8-9.

23. Sonnichsen, *Pass of the North*, Vol. 1, pp. 236-237.

24. Metz, *Dallas Stoudenmire*, pp. 91, 95.

Dallas Stoudenmire (1945—1882) succeeded George W. Campbell and William Johnson as city marshal of El Paso in 1881. (Courtesy of Bob McNellis.)

5

Dallas Stoudenmire

As George's affairs achieved a temporary equilibrium, with or without the Mannings, a new series of events across the river brought him closer to the end of his career. On January 28, 1881, action was initiated by the gang of seven rowdy Americans whom Campbell and the Rangers had forced to leave town.[1] The catalyst was a Mexican peddler who had indulged in too much tequila. George Look describes the almost-comic scene:

> A peddler came into a dance-hall over the river and displayed some money. The gang of Americans took him out, held him up 3 or 4 times; each time, he would come back and display some more money, so they finally took him out, stripped him, and got something like $800 from him. The day following this hold-up the Mexican authorities over the river arrested every American over there— played no favorites to anyone. The jail was full of American boys.[2]

Some innocent men were picked up, but eventually only the ones involved were retained in jail. The records of the American consul in Paso del Norte indicate that they were

Frank Thompson, Frank O'Neal, J. C. Cain, Les Davis, Patrick Ryan, Frank Allen, and Hugh Cox.[3] George Look recalled them as Nibsy, Thompson, Lafayette Kid, Ryan, and Joe King. Shortly after their arrest, according to Ranger Beaumont, a Mexican brought a note to the company quarters. It read, "Boys, we are in the Mexican jail. We are as hungry as it is possible to be. Please send us some chuck." That, said Beaumont, "was enough for us, and we took turns going the rounds of the eating houses of El Paso, and every day carried them food, and now and then a little money. We kept this up for about a week and then the sporting men took the job off our hands."[4]

When two more weeks has passed and no trial had been scheduled, an escape plan was developed by the prisoners. The prisoners had heard rumors that they would be moved to Chihuahua and they feared that they would be shot enroute.[5] By this time, some Mexican girl friends of the prisoners were delivering the food. "One day," Beaumont continued, "they carried them an army bucket filled with soup. In the bucket they placed three loaded guns. They buried the guns in the dirt floor of their cell and passed the bucket out to the Mexicans. During the day the prisoners were allowed to walk around the jail yard. The next day, February 18, 1881, at 8:30 a.m., after the door of their cell was opened, they sprang to the main entrance, shot down the two guards and ran out onto the plaza."

Frank Thompson, carrying one of the guns, led the escape. He shot the captain at the gate through the stomach and killed the other guard. He then walked up and down in front of the jail entrance calling for the others to come out. He was soon joined by Frank (Nibsy) O'Neal and J. C. Cain with the other guns. Patrick (Paddy) Ryan and the Lafayette Kid, both unarmed, hesitated but eventually came out. Cox and Davis evidently made no attempt to escape. Feeling himself defenseless, Ryan lost his nerve, ran into the saloon on the corner, hid behind the bar, and was later apprehended there. The Lafayette Kid got half-way down the hill, where he tripped, fell into the gutter, and lay there till he was arrested and taken back to jail. Thompson, O'Neal and Cain ran across the fields north of the jail and made it to the *acequia* (irrigation ditch) two or three blocks away.

Meanwhile, as the break started, a Mexican vaquero was having breakfast in a restaurant on the plaza opposite the jail. His horse with his Winchester on the saddle was tied outside. On hearing the shots he ran out, mounted, overtook the fugitives, and opened fire. The boys fired back at him and there was a brisk exchange of shots. The Winchester was the better weapon, however, and the vaquero picked them off one after the other as they tried to cross the *acequia*. The three bodies floated down to the bridge below and were fished out. Each body was tied to the tail of a burro. George Look was a witness and described the macabre scene, "They were a horrible looking sight. They rolled around and around in the dust as they hauled them up to headquarters back of the old church."

As soon as the news reached El Paso, several residents crossed the river and asked for the bodies. The Mexicans asked

$75 each for them. Nobody had that much money, so the men were buried in a ditch, in one grave, without any boxes.[6]

The escape took place on February 18, 1881. Almost exactly three months later Paddy Ryan, Les (Lou) Davis and Frank Allen (possibly Lafayette Kid) made a second and successful attempt. Hugh Cox, who was too ill to join them, obtained a medical release in September.[7]

The treatment of these prisoners did not set well with many Americans in El Paso. Old animosities were ready to flare up again, and some of the Anglos were watching for an opportunity to get even, especially with the vaquero with the Winchester. The Mexicans were aware of these feelings and were especially cautious.

At about this time, George Campbell went over to Paso del Norte, and the Mexican officers attempted to arrest him for carrying arms. He had to run for the American side to stay out of trouble.[8] Resentment over this incident was still smoldering in him a month later when everything came to a climax. No first-hand record of his feelings exist, but later newspaper articles offer a few clues. He was evidently becoming disillusioned with life in El Paso and was planning to move. John Hampton reported in the *Ashland Independent* not long afterwards, "I find in his trunk letters from the present sheriff [at Henrietta] requesting him to come back and accept the office again. Also, letters from some of the best citizens of that county showing that they held him in high esteem, being friendly correspondents." The *Henrietta Shield* noted that "A letter received from him on the

The Mexican jail at Paso del Norte in about 1880. The main gate and guards are in the area behind the lamp post. This is the prison from which the Texans escaped. The escapees reached the acequia near the tree tops that are visible between the jail and saloon. Paddy Ryan took refuge in the saloon. Mount Franklin of El Paso is visible in the background. (Courtesy of the author.)

day of his death said that he expected to start home in a short time, coming to Henrietta,-and thence to Kentucky to live with his brother."[9]

Unexpected events interfered with his plans. Doc Cummings, who had arrived on about the first of the year of 1881 and had opened the Globe Restaurant, had succeeded in persuading his brother-in-law, Dallas Stoudenmire, to leave Socorro, New Mexico, and come to El Paso in April. Dallas was a formidable specimen, thirty-five years old, six feet two, weighing 180 pounds, with auburn hair, and hazel eyes. He was a Confederate veteran and an ex-Texas Ranger who had tried farming and sheepraising in East Texas, but he did not seem inclined toward peaceful pursuits. He had killed a man in Colorado County, Texas in 1876, and possibly two more at Alleyton in 1878.[10] His record included a number of gunfights which occurred when he was not on duty as either a soldier or lawman. Just before his arrival in El Paso, he had been marshal of Socorro, New Mexico.[11] His duties required him to spend much of his time in the saloons and in the tenderloin, and he had developed a fondness for whiskey and red-light girls.

Cummings seems to have laid the groundwork well. On April 11, 1881, Bill Johnson was asked to resign as marshal of El Paso, and Stoudenmire was sworn in despite substantial but unidentified defects in his bond pointed out by Alderman James Hague.[12] The very next day the Mexican-American pot began to boil.

The fire was lighted by Don Ynocente Ochoa, a wealthy

The benches to the left in the plaza of Paso del Norte where George Look was sitting when he saw "three or four burros with a man's body tied to the tail of each, dragging them through the dust." The bodies were hauled to the headquarters and jail back of the church. The Our Lady of Guadalupe Mission still stands at this location in Juarez, Mexico, alongside a newer cathedral. (Courtesy of the Aultman Collection, El Paso Public Library.)

merchant who, like Mayor Schutz, had stores on both sides of the river. He lodged a complaint with both Mayor Schutz and Captain Baylor; he said he was missing thirty head of cattle from his Mexican ranch and claimed that the trail led directly to Johnny Hale's corrals. Private Ed Fitch of the Rangers was assigned to take ten of Ochoa's vaqueros and recover the herd.[13] Fitch found only three head, and Hale indignantly claimed that he had bought them. A heated argument ensued, Hale claiming that he was being slandered and insulted.

The posse left empty-handed, but two young Mexicans remained behind to conduct a search of their own. Their names (misspelled by the Americans) were Gilberto Jaurique and Jose Sanchez.[14] They came from good families and George Look believed that one of them was the vaquero who had killed the three American escapees two months before.[15] They were surprised and killed by two Americans, former-Ranger Chris Peveler and Frank Stevenson. The *El Paso Herald* of April 13, 1881, carried the story: "News came today of the killing of two Mexicans eleven miles above the city, by Lum Peabody [Chris Peveler] and Frank Stevenson, who surrendered themselves and were brought to the city."

There were two versions of what had happened. The killers' story, as related by Ranger Beaumont, was that when they went after their horses that morning and found them missing, they "soon found a trail that ran towards the river bank. They found their horses and two Mexicans riding them. They asked no questions and soon they had their horses and the Mexicans had gone the one way trail."[16]

Ynocente Ochoa, the Merchant Prince of Paso del Norte.

Captain Baylor had a different story. "Mr. Warren Phillips one of our aldermen tells me he saw the ground a short time after the killing and it was plain to him that the young Mexicans had stopped under a shade to eat and smoke and their assailants had crept up and killed them both."[17] When word of the killings reached Mexico, it created a great furor among the citizens of Paso del Norte and it became apparent immediately that serious consequence might result.

On April 14, 1881, two days after Sr. Ochoa had made his complaint, newly appointed Marshal Stoudenmire and Ranger Frank Beaumont were standing at the corner of El Paso and San Antonio Streets, the crossroads of the town. As Beaumont remembered it, "Stoudenmire had been looking towards the river for some time. He finally said: 'Frank, what do you think causes all that dust on the river bank?' I looked in the same direction, and soon we saw a large number of horses turning into El Paso Street. On they came until at least 50 heavily armed Mexicans passed by us [George Look estimated the number to be seventy-five or eighty]. We hurried after them and found them in front of the mayor's office on San Franicsco Street."

It was at this point that Stoudenmire found himself at odds with the mayor, just as George Campbell had been. Ranger Beaumont continues:

Two of the leaders were about to enter the office of mayor Solomon Schultz [sic]. We went in with them and Stoudenmire said: "Mr. Mayor, what is the cause of these

Looking south on El Paso Street from the balcony of the
Central Hotel in about October-November of 1881.
Stoudenmire and Beaumont were looking in this direction
when they saw the dust rising from eighty armed Mexicans
as they rode across the Rio Grande near the horizon. San
Francisco Street is to the right. (Courtesy of Millard G.
McKinney.)

armed greasers being in El Paso?" "They are friends of
mine," replied the mayor, "and I am going to give them
permission to carry arms in the state. They are going after those two young men that were killed yesterday."
"Who the devil do you think you are anyway?" said the
marshal. "You had better advise your friends to leave at
once, or it will take another crowd to cart these greasers
home." After making some inquiries we thought best to
let them go. They took a wagon with them and Gus Krin-
craw [Krempkau] a man from San Antonio, went with
them."[18]

The mayor had his way and the party left, guided by
Krempkau, a former Ranger who may have been newly deputized as a city constable.

Once they were out of sight, the men of El Paso began to
gather in the streets, indignant at the insolence of the Mexicans.
Some were in favor of following them and cleaning out the
whole crowd. Wiser counsels prevailed, however, and gradually
things quieted down until midafternoon, when the Mexicans returned with the dead men. "As soon as it was known that the
Mexicans had returned," Beaumont continues, "in less than 10
minutes El Paso Street was lined with armed men."[19] They
watched as the posse gathered across from Judge J. A. Buckler's
office near the San Antonio-El Paso Street intersection, where
an inquest was under way. Gus Krempkau was interpreting and
G. F. Neill was serving as prosecuting attorney. Outside, tension

was building up. Ben Schuster, looking on from his store directly across the street, saw the danger and tried to persuade both sides to turn in their arms. When he failed to get any response, he went to Attorney Neill and pointed out the mounting danger. As a result, the Mexicans were allowed to move the wagon containing the bodies to a point farther south on El Paso Street and the proceedings were speeded up.[20]

NOTES

1. *El Paso Herald*, November 13, 1909.

2. Look, George, "Reminiscences."

3. Metz, *Dallas Stoudenmire*, pp. 22-23, quoting a letter of Charles Richardson, U. S. State Department, October 14, 1881.

4. *El Paso Herald*, November 13, 1909.

5. *Galveston News*, February 19, 1881.

6. Look, "Reminiscences."

7. Richardson's report is quoted in Metz, *Dallas Stoudenmire*, pp. 22-23. F. Stanley in *The San Marcial Story*. White Deer, Texas: Pvt. ptd., 1960, p. 9, quoting a San Marcial paper for June 23, 1881, says that "Paddy Ryan, who escaped El Paso del Norte jail, shot and killed Chas. Walker, city marshal of San Marcial here this evening. He fired six shots, five of them lodged in a space that could be covered by the hand—directly over the heart. Walker was a good officer. Ryan ran for the mountains pursued by a large body of men. He never returned to San Marcial nor was he ever captured."

8. *Ashland Independent*, [May, 1881].

9. *Henrietta Shield*, [April, 1881].

10. O'Neal, Bill, *Encyclopedia of Western Gunfighters.* Norman: University of Oklahoma Press, 1979, pp. 302-305.

11. Socorro, New Mexico, court records, checked by Bob McNellis.

12. Metz, *Dallas Stoudenmire*, Chapter I.

13. Captain G. W. Baylor to General W. H. King, September 30, 1881, Adjutant General's Office Papers, Barker History Center, Austin.

14. *Chicago Tribune*, April 16, 1881.

15. Look, "Reminiscences," p. 3.

16. *El Paso Herald*, November 13, 1909.

17. Captain G. W. Baylor, letter to General W. H. King, September 30, 1881. Adjutant General's Office Papers, Barker History Center, Austin.

18. *El Paso Herald*, November 13, 1909.

19. Look, "Reminiscences," p. 3.

20. Look, "Reminiscences," p. 3.

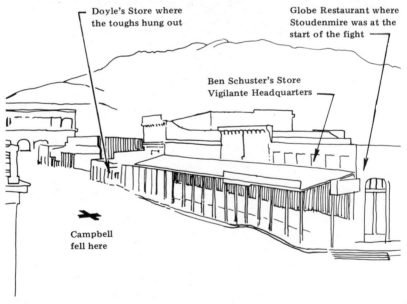

Doyle's Store where
the toughs hung out

Globe Restaurant where
Stoudenmire was at the
start of the fight

Ben Schuster's Store
Vigilante Headquarters

Campbell
fell here

This photograph and drawing show the east side of El Paso Street from the intersection with Overland Street. The drawing is labeled to show the identities of the buildings and the locations of the street fight. (photo courtesy of Millard J. McKinney.)

6

The Shoot-Out

The brief but bloody drama which then unfolded has been described in a dozen different ways over the years. In outline, however, the stories are consistent, particularly those which appeared in newspapers within a day or two of the event. Perhaps the most trustworthy of all was written by John W. Hampton, using the report of the State's (District) Attorney, which was actually a description of the gunfight by George Campbell, the only participant from beginning to end who lived long enough to tell about it. Hampton had been sent to El Paso by George's brother Abe to search out the facts of the tragedy. His account was printed in the *Ashland Independent* within a week or two of the event.[1] The article follows:

Full Account of the Death of G. W. Campbell

Editor, *Independent*—On the 13th of April, 1881, two Mexicans were killed near one Hale's cattle ranch a few miles from El Paso. Two young men came in and surrendered themselves for trial stating that they had killed the Mexicans, that they had been waylaid by them and shot at, but the Mexicans missing they had killed them.

This statement Hale and two men on his ranch confirmed. The Mexicans lived on the Mexican side of the Rio Grande, and 'tis said by the citizens there that they were nice young men, brothers, and had gone to look for some cattle which had been stolen from them. The character of Hale and his ranch was bad. So that I found that the prevailing opinion was that the two Mexicans had been murdered.

. . . .

Some of the authorities on the Mexican side applied for the bodies, and this request was granted. The bodies of the Mexicans had been brought to the city, the inquest was being held and the armed Mexicans were in line on the street. The inquest was being held in the justice's office.

A short time before this, the police of the city of El Paso on the Mexican side had attempted to arrest Campbell for carrying arms and he had to skip to the American side to avoid arrest. Seeing this armed force of Mexicans on the streets of an American city raised his ire, and he, in substance and the most forcible language said, that the bodies of the Mexicans should have been delivered to their friends on the border by the American authorities—that America was able to take care of itself, that the precedent was a bad one, that they might claim it as a right in the future, that now there were enough armed foreigners in their streets to take the town.

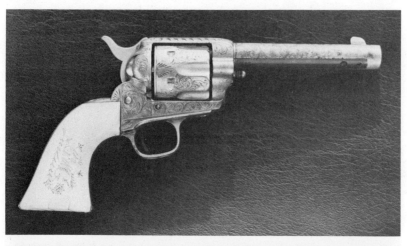

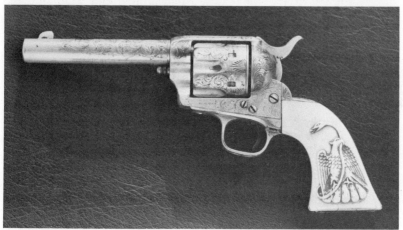

Geroge Washington Campbell was carrying this gun when he was killed by Stoudenmire. It is a silver-plated, engraved Colt .45 single action with carved and inscribed ivory grips, serial number 22,459. For some reason the initials on the grips are "CWG" instead of "GWC." (Courtesy of George V. Campbell and Fred Egloff.)

He said that none but a set of scalawag Jews such as had control of that town would have thought of allowing such an indignity, but true to their instinct, having sold their Saviour for thirty pieces of silver, they would now sell their country for the purpose of currying favor and securing trade.

No one at the time seemed to take any offense at this. But someone told Knowcamp [Krempkau], who was not a Jew, that Campbell had been using epithets of an opprobrious character toward him for going to get the bodies of the Mexicans. He was mad and went out and hunted Campbell up. Found him sitting in a store, called him out and in a very excited manner told him what he had heard. Campbell said that he had said nothing that would reflect upon his conduct, but that on the contrary he had done right to go and get the bodies, that it was the presence of the armed Mexican force that he objected to. This Knowcamp [Krempkau], said was satisfactory. But Hale being mad because Knowcamp [Krempkau] had gone to his ranch for the bodies, and having witnessed the altercation, but not being close enough to hear what was said came up and drew his revolver on Knowcamp [Krempkau] and told Campbell to draw that he had him covered. Campbell said that it was not his fight and started away, seeing that there would be an encounter. Hale and Knowcamp [Krempkau] had commenced shooting about the same time. Hale fell at once against a pillar with a death wound, but kept on shooting. Knowcamp [Krempkau] received a death wound at first, but stood on his feet and shot several times. One or the other of these wounded men shot Campbell in the foot as he was walking across the street. About this time, the marshal, Stubenmyer [*sic*] came running up and shot at Hale and killed a Mexican standing further on down the street, and then fired at Campbell and broke his right arm. At this Campbell attempted to draw his revolver with his left hand and Stubenmyer [*sic*] again shot him through which felled him to the ground. This was about six o'clock, P. M. and he died about five o'clock the next morning. He was perfectly rational up to the second before he died. He made his dying declaration in the presence of the State's Attorney, in which he stated the facts as I have given them above. Said that he did not want to have any difficulty, that he understood Knowcamp [Krempkau] to accept the explanation.

Supposed that Hale seeing the excited manner in which Knowcamp [Krempkau] was talking to him supposed that he would find a confederate in him (Campbell). He said that he was doing nothing, was trying to get out of danger, that he had not said or done anything to the marshal, and that the marshal did not call on any one to desist or surrender but commenced shooting in the manner above stated.

He died like a hero and never groaned or mur-
mured from the time he was wounded till he died. He has
a great many warm friends in the town, and a large ma-
jority of the people there think that he was cruelly murdered and so express themselves on the streets. The examining trial was to come off on the 27th ult. What was
done we have not learned, but I employed able counsel to
assist the Commonwealth's Attorney.

John W. Hampton

The two people who claimed to have witnessed the gunfight wrote about it twenty to thirty years later. W. W. Mills,
writing in 1901, said that Campbell and Krempkau were sober
and that Hale was intoxicated. Krempkau and Campbell fired
simultaneously, killing each other. His substitution of Campbell
for Hale confused historians for years.[2] George Look, writing in
1909, stated that Hale started the affair and killed Krempkau,
who in return killed Hale. "Campbell," he says, "ducked out
into the middle of the street shouting, 'It isn't my fight.' " After being shot down, George "looked up at Studemier [sic] and
says, 'You big son of a ——, you murdered me!' "[3]

Two people who did not see the shooting were close
enough to write about it. Merchant Zach White heard the shots,
was worried for the safety of his employees, and stepped outside. He caught a glimpse of the street littered with bodies, but
stumbled back behind an adobe pillar when Stoudenmire glared

W. W. Mills, witness to the 1881 shootout who wrote of it in his book FORTY YEARS IN EL PASO, admitted that he knew little of Campbell and told how John Hale once befriended him. Mills warned his readers that, "Much that I was tempted to write has been omitted out of consideration for the living and the dead and their relatives." (Courtesy of Millard G. McKinney.)

at him and roared, "You S. O. B., stand back!"[4] Ranger Beaumont had left the scene moments before to investigate the report of a row on San Francisco Street. He had heard Campbell and Krempkau come to an understanding and reported seeing Hale, as drunk as it was possible to be heading down El Paso Street. By the time he was able to get back, the fight was over. "We carried Campbell to a room in the Overland Building," Beaumont wrote. "Everything that friends and doctors could do was done. Death had set its seal upon him."[5]

News of the slaughter reached the outside world very quickly, and newspapers in many parts of the country carried the news. The *Chicago Daily News* on April 15, 1881, ran a sensational report reprinted from the *Kansas City Evening Star*. It credited Krempkau with an amazing shot: "Hale fired and killed Krempkau, a policemen, who fired at the same time, wounding the newly elected Marshal Stoudenmire, and killed Hale and a Mexican bystander with the same shot. Campbell, a friend of Hale, attempted to draw a pistol and was mortally wounded by Stoudenmire." The *Chicago Tribune* and the *Daily Interocean* carried accounts the following day.

A number of discrepancies appeared in these stories. One involved the shot which killed Hale. Stoudenmire said he fired it. Later on, when he was drunk, he would sometimes set up targets in the street and recreate the gunfight.[6] He had to claim the killing of Hale to justify his actions.

There is doubt also about whether or not George was armed. Ranger Beaumont says he was not, but his statement is

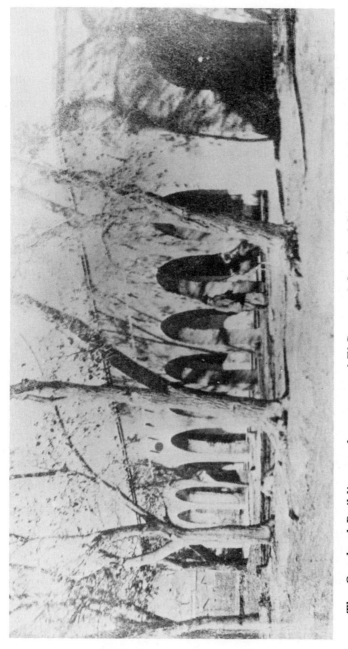

The Overland Building at the corner of El Paso and Overland Streets was the headquarters of the Texas Rangers. George Campbell was carried to this building after the gunfight and died here the next morning. (Courtesy of the Aultman Collection, The El Paso Public Library.)

highly suspect. Some reports say that Stoudenmire shot Campbell's pistol out of his right hand. This would have been impossible, for the existing tintype of George, when reversed to give the correct image, shows that he was left-handed, wearing his gun in a cross-draw position. The *Henrietta Shield*, quoting from news dispatches, accepts the story that "The marshal claims that George was about drawing his pistol to fight for a friend, and thereupon he fired and George fell."[7] If this story is correct, George was armed, but had not drawn his pistol when he was fatally shot.

The events which followed immediately after Campbell's death are related in a letter written by District Attorney G. F. Neill.

El Paso, Texas

April 20, 1881

Hon. W. B. Plemons, Henrietta, Texas

My Dear Sir,—Your friend, G. W. Campbell, was shot and killed here on the 15th Inst., by the city marshal, Dallas Stoudenmire. Mr. Campbell lived till the morning of the 15th. He was buried as well as he could have been in this place and his funeral was well attended as he had many friends here. He has been taken up and his body embalmed and will be sent to Kentucky for final burial. Mr. Wm. Gilson was with him during his last moments and deeply mourns the loss of his best friend.

I am, &c, your obd't servant,   G. F. Neill[8]

The west side of El Paso Street looking north from the top of the Overland Building. The April 14, 1881, shoot-out took place where the adobe portico ends (right of center in the photograph). John Hale fell behind the corner pillar. Gus Krempkau fell at the front door of Keating's Saloon on this side of the portico. (Courtesy of Millard G. McKinney.)

The only William Gilson known to have been around El Paso at that time was a young reputable Irish immigrant employed by the railroad.[9] The fact that Campbell had some Irish blood may have fostered the friendship. It is interesting to note that Campbell's best friend was not one of the Mannings.

The question which arose in many men's minds at this stage asked: Was Stoudenmire guilty of murder, and if so, why was he not arrested and held for trial? One reason, of course, was that the mayor and council had no love for Campbell and they backed their man, Stoudenmire. Another was the fact that J. W. Hampton, who might have led the cry for justice, was on the train, taking the body back to Kentucky.[10] Another was fear of consequences. Feeling was running high on both sides. Mayor Schutz found this an opportune time to leave town on a trip back East that lasted seven weeks. Although Stoudenmire had been marshal for less than a week, he had proved that he was not to be trifled with, and most men, including the mayor, were not about to trifle with him. Dallas had a short fuse which seemed to be getting shorter. The events which took place between the gun battle and the examining trial made the point. Bill, Johnson, Stoudenmire's predecessor and now his deputy, touched the match to the powder keg

Ranger Beaumont was standing with Johnson in front of the Manning saloon on El Paso street when it happened:

The new marshal came up and said: "Johnson, I want the key to the jail." Johnson drew a ring from his pocket

No. 44.

HALF RATE MESSAGES.

THE WESTERN UNION TELEGRAPH COMPANY.

This Company **TRANSMITS** and **DELIVERS** messages only on conditions, limiting its liability, which have been assented to by the sender of the following message.
Errors can be guarded against only by repeating a message back to the sending station for comparison, and the Company will not hold itself liable for errors or delays in transmission or delivery of **Unrepeated Messages.**
This message is an **UNREPEATED MESSAGE** and is delivered by request of the sender under the conditions named above.

A. R. BREWER, Sec'y.   NORVIN GREEN, President.

Dated *El Paso, Tex* *15th* 188*1*

Received at *Ashland, Ky. 8½ April 15*

To *A. O. Campbell*

Your Brother was shot and killed here yesterday

J. A. Buckler

9 Pai O'clock 6 3+25

Via Denison

Tex

READ THE NOTICE AT THE TOP.

with two keys that looked exactly alike and said, "Dallas, one of these keys belongs to my stable. I will go home soon and see which is the right one and bring it to you." Stoudenmire snatched the keys from Johnson's hand and said, "Damn you, I want them now. What the devil are you going to do about it?" No trouble took place at the time and the marshal soon passed down the street.[11]

Johnson spent the day drowning his anger with booze. About an hour after sunset, thoroughly soused and armed with a shotgun, he sat on and slightly behind a pile of bricks on San Antonio Street. Soon Stoudenmire and Doc Cummings approached from the direction of the Acme Saloon farther east on San Antonio. When they were within twenty-five feet, Johnson demanded his key and let fly with both barrels. The alcohol and his crippled arm didn't help his marksmanship, and he missed completely. The marshal promptly filled him full of lead. He was hit at least nine times and died instantly.[12] Reports circulated later that shots were then fired at Stoudenmire from the direction of Manning's saloon. Stoudenmire received a heel wound and retired to the Ranger camp at Ysleta to recover.

Doc Cummings felt that it was now time for him to take a hand. He organized and led a vigilante group which threatened the lives of all people whom he considered enemies. During the following week this group planned a surprise party—a mass execution of the crowd which frequented Doyle's saloon. Ben Schuster opposed the plan, pointing out that a lot of innocent

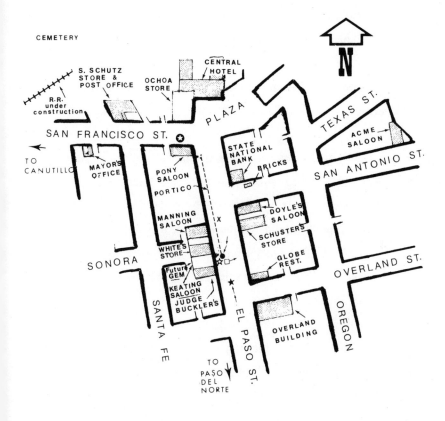

CEMETERY

S. SCHUTZ STORE & POST OFFICE

OCHOA STORE

CENTRAL HOTEL

R.R. under construction

PLAZA

SAN FRANCISCO ST.

TEXAS ST.

ACME SALOON

SAN ANTONIO ST.

TO CANUTILLO

MAYOR'S OFFICE

PONY SALOON

PORTICO

STATE NATIONAL BANK

BRICKS

MANNING SALOON

DOYLE'S SALOON

SCHUSTER'S STORE

OVERLAND ST.

WHITE'S STORE

GLOBE REST.

SONORA

Future GEM

KEATING SALOON

JUDGE BUCKLER'S

SANTA FE

EL PASO ST.

OREGON

OVERLAND BUILDING

TO PASO DEL NORTE

N

EL PASO

APRIL 14, 1881

TIME : 5:30 - 6 PM

LOCATIONS INVOLVED

SOURCE : CONKLIN MAP NOV 1881

KEY

STOUDENMIRE	★
CAMPBELL	☐
KREMPKAU	☆
HALE	●
PEREZ (bystander)	X
RANGERS	✪

people would be killed.[13] Besides, the Rangers had moved in again, and the shootup was dropped. The vigilantes continued their campaign of intimidation, however, forcing people to leave town.[14]

Stoudenmire returned to El Paso, replacing Baylor, April 24, 1881. The hearing was held three days later. By that time it would have been difficult to find anyone in town willing to express an opinion different from the marshal's, let alone appear at a hearing. The verdict, consequently, was as follows:

> We, the jury, agree that Gus Krempkau came to his death by a pistol shot fired by John Hale, and Campbell and Hale came to their deaths by pistol shots fired by the City Marshall, Dallas Stoudenmire, in executing his duty as marshal of the city of El Paso.—Albert Schutz, Paul W. Keating, Tobias Freilweek, Jas. Scharcher, John Evens, Henry Walton.[15]

An indication that many disagreed with this verdict occupies the very last page of the Campbell family scrapbook in the form of a letter written by Judge J. A. Buckler and sent to Abe Campbell almost a year and half after George's death:

LAW OFFICE OF J. A. BUCKLER   El Paso, Texas

                                                             Sept. 19, 1882

Mr. Abe Campbell
Ashland, Kentucky

Dallas Stoudenmire's "belly gun" that he used as a concealed gun in his belt. This gun was taken from Stoudenmire's body when he was killed in 1882. (Courtesy of Gordon Frost and Leon C. Metz.)

Dear Sir: Time at last sets all things even. George's murderer was shot and killed here yesterday afternoon by Jim Manning. There were two of the Manning boys engaged in the difficulty, but it is not certain which one did the killing which was justifiable. Stoudenmire had been turned out of office of Marshal some months ago by the City Council and has ever since been quarreling with the Mannings whenever he got drunk. He shot Dr. Manning through the arm before he was killed. I will send you a full report if one be published in the newspaper.

Yours very truly, J. A. Buckler

Some excuse, it is true, can be made for Stoudenmire. To give him the benefit of some rather large doubts, it must be acknowledged that he was under extreme pressure at the time of the shootout. He was the new marshal in town who wanted to establish himself as the authority. He plunged into a brawl he did not understand, with consequences he could not foresee, and he was operating on the theory that violence must be met with violence.

How effective was he as a peace officer? The answer depends on how well he succeeded in bringing law and order to a lawless town.

Campbell, on the other hand, apparently tried to keep the lid on by persuasion rather than by violence. This could be, and was, interpreted as being too friendly with the wrong people. There are indications that he did not return the affection, if

such friendships existed, and it must be remembered that sometimes it is hard to distinguish between affection and respect.[16]
Unfortunately, the New Year's Eve riot, which was the marshal's job to prevent, destroys some of George's credit. His
threats against the mayor's life, along with his anti-Semitic re-
marks, does him further damage, but during the month and a
half he held the marshal's office there was no homicide that has
come to light.

Stoudenmire, in contrast, must answer for seven homicides during his first week in office. The unnecessary deaths of
Campbell and Perez (the innocent bystander killed during the
shootout) would not have taken place had it not been for his
overreaction. He was able to stay in office for a year, consider-
ably longer than any of his predecessors, but that year is stained
with homicides and near-fatal encounters. At first he received a
great deal of assistance from the Texas Rangers, but this abrupt-
ly stopped when he began feuding with them. Unlike Campbell,
he received a good salary, and he had four assistants, but despite
all of this, violence continued. Matters grew worse until he treed
the entire city council at one of their meetings.[17] This incident
led to his resignation, and he died in a gunfight that he himself
had instigated. The city seemed relieved to hear of his death. His
assistant, Jim Gillett, succeeded him and did a far better job of
establishing law and order at the Pass.

Unlike Stoudenmire, George Campbell was sincerely
mourned. Judge W. B. Plemons wrote to the Campbell family
on May 1, 1881: "Poor boy, his fate was a sad one, but you and

his relatives can rest assured of one thing, which is, that while he lived he did nothing that reflected on his good name and he died respected by those who had known him for years. His death cast a gloom over our entire town of Henrietta, and strong and brave men unconsciously shed tears over his fate."[18] The *Henrietta Shield* echoed these sentiments with the headline, A BRAVE MAN GONE.[19]

"Time sets all things even," said Judge Buckler. It has taken a full century for the balance to be restored in the case of George Campbell, but he should do better in public estimation from now on.

NOTES

1. *Ashland Independent*, May, 1881.

2. Mills, *Forty Years at El Paso*, pp. 161-162.

3. Look, "Reminiscences," p. 4.

4. *El Paso Evening Post*, May 30, 1928 (Zach White's story).

5. *El Paso Herald*, November 27, 1909.

6. Metz, *Dallas Stoudenmire*, p. 126.

7. *Henrietta Shield*, [April, 1881].

8. George W. Campbell letters, in possession of George V. Campbell.

9. William Gilson, interview with FRE, El Paso, Texas.

10. *Ashland Independent*, [May, 1881].

11. *El Paso Herald*, November 27, 1909.

12. Look, "Reminiscences," p. 5.

13. Look, "Reminiscences," p. 5.

14. *Newman's Semi-Weekly*, April 20, 1881.

15. *El Paso Herald*, December 28, 1881, quoting from the previous issue.

16. *El Paso Herald*, November 13, 1909; *Ashland Independent*, May, 1881.

17. Metz, *Dallas Stoudenmire*, p. 106.

18. Judge W. B. Plemons to Abe Campbell, Henrietta, Texas, May 1, 1881.

19. *Henrietta Shield*, [May, 1881].

The northeast corner of San Antonio and El Paso Streets where Johnson was killed April 17, 1881. Bill Johnson was standing this side of the brick pile when he ambushed Dallas Stoudenmire, missed his shot, and was killed by Stoudenmire. (Courtesy of Millard G. McKinney.)

Dallas Stoudenmire, the gunfighting marshal of El Paso, Texas.

7
Aftermath

The death of George Campbell played a significant part in a chain of events and bitter feelings that eventually led to Stoudenmire's demise. It was by no means the sole factor involved but a fine line of cause and effect is present. The remainder of Dallas Stoudenmire's days were anything but tranquil. In all fairness he must be credited with some examples of good law enforcement and detective work. A combination of alcoholism and feuding proved to be his undoing.

Alcohol was undoubtedly his greatest weakness. The extent and nature of his problem only became apparent to the citizens of El Paso after he had resided there awhile. Parson Tays was one who paid heed to the marshal's drinking habits when he alluded to them in a Sunday sermon. That night the inebriated and enraged city marshal shot up the church bell on St. Clements church.[1]

Stoudenmire started out on relatively friendly terms with the Texas Rangers. He enlisted their aid and even paid a few dollars bounty to them for their making arrests. Doc Cummings, his brother-in-law, even served as a Ranger for a month or so. The friendship that many of the Rangers exhibited toward the Manning brothers evidently led to a parting of the ways. Capt. Baylor's efforts to check the criminal record of "Mysterious

Dave" Mather (Who may have served as an assistant marshal using an alias) also fueled the fire.[2] Soon Stoudenmire was labeling the Rangers as cowards and accusing them of causing more harm than good, and this feud continued to grow even after Baylor's son-in-law Jim Gillett became an Assistant City Marshal in December of 1881.

Dallas Stoudenmire and Doc Cummings directed their greatest wrath against Jim and Frank Manning who were joined by Dr. Felix Manning. Another brother by the name of John appears not to have been very much involved with the feud. Dallas and Doc became obsessed with the idea that the Mannings were inciting people against them and were responsible for the fatal April outbursts. Oral accounts among Manning descendants reveal that the feud may have begun even before the El Paso days.[3] It is known that Jim Manning was angered by the death of his friend George Campbell whom he thought had been murdered by Stoudenmire. Although no tie with the Mannings was ever made, a tough by the name of Joe King tried to ambush Stoudenmire on the night of December 16, 1881. He only succeeded in temporarily blinding the marshal with the gunflash. In turn Stoudenmire seems to have gone out of his way to antagonize the Mannings. Court records list numerous and repetitive arrests on petty charges.[4] Stoudenmire's drunken reenactments of the April gunfight also appeared as a taunt.

The pent-up hatred erupted early in 1882. A Kansas sheriff arrived in El Paso early in February. He was trailing a rapist who escaped into Mexico and was evidently headed for Chihuahua. Doc Cummings, always the police buff, volunteered to assist, he was promptly deputized, and headed into Mexico with the Kansas lawman. During his absence Dallas Stoudenmire also left town to wed Miss Isabella Sherrington at Columbus, Texas. Jim Gillett was left in charge of the El Paso police. A week later Cummings returned to El Paso from a futile manhunt. While in Mexico, Cummings had seen George Campbell's best friend, Bill Gilson, who was there working on the Mexican railroad.[5] What they said to each other remains unrecorded, but the meeting was evidently not cordial. It did, however, succeed in fanning Doc's smoldering resentment against the Mannings.

Finding Gillett confined to bed with influenza, Cummings mistakenly assumed he had official sanction because of his recent duty as a deputy. He stuck two .45 pistols in his front pants pockets, had a few drinks at the Old Boss saloon, and said he was going to "clean the damned Mannings up." It was 6:30, February 14, 1882, when a booze-brave Cummings headed for Manning's Coliseum Variety Theater. He found Jim Manning in the bar room. In an obvious attempt to provoke trouble, he asked Jim to take a drink, knowing full well that Manning was on the wagon. Jim avoided falling for the ploy by agreeing to have a glass of cider.

Cumming's then brought up his meeting with Gilson in Mexico and accused Manning of encouraging Johnson in his unsuccessful assassination attempt on Stoudenmire. Manning told him he was mistaken. "You're a God damn liar," retorted Cummings. He continued to argue and bait Manning on a number of subjects, finally asking if Jim was armed. Jim replied that he wasn't armed, he didn't want trouble, and matters could be settled in a peaceful way. He even offered to get down on his knees if necessary. Cumming's called him a coward and began arguing with J. C. Kling, the bartender. Manning told him to leave the bartender out of it and convinced Doc to step outside. Once they were in the street Doc grabbed Jim by the collar and said, "I think that I will kill you now!" At that instant he was distracted by an innocent passerby. He turned on the fellow, called him an S. O. B., threatened him with his gun, and made him walk off with his hands raised.

Jim Manning went back inside the Coliseum while Cummings was distracted by the passerby. Moments later Doc stormed back in to find him. He warned bartender Kling to keep his hands on the bar, and Kling denied having a gun. Jim Manning then stepped into an adjoining hall for a moment. He returned to the doorway wearing a pistol and said, "Doc, we will have this out." Doc had a drink in his hand and thus was slow to draw. He was hit by two bullets as he got off one wild shot. Someone hit Cummings on the head with a gun barrel and he plunged thru the front door and fell in El Paso street. One of the fatal shots was from Manning's gun, the other was most likely fired by Kling. According to Jim Gillett, "It was generally understood that a barkeeper of Mannings really did the shooting." Jim Manning assumed the responsibility for the killing and was turned loose when a *habeas corpus* proceedings found his action justified.

Jim Manning in 1889 when he owned a liquor store in Seattle, Washington. (Courtesy of Frank Manning and Leon Metz.)

Stoudenmire returned to El Paso with his new bride on February 25, 1882. Gillett met him at the train and informed him that his brother-in-law had been killed and filled him in on the details. Gillett remembered that Dallas, "made no effort to conceal his feelings said if the Mannings wanted a fight they could get it."[6] He began to hit the bottle more than ever. Dr. E. H. Irvin recalled that "He would sit for hours, drinking, and manuevering his guns, spinning the cylinders, practicing a fast draw."[7]

A month had barely passed when an editorial appeared in *The Lone Star* dealing with law and order and comparing El Paso to a volcano about to erupt. On that same day, March 25, the City Council placed assistant marshal Gillett in charge of the city police noting that marshal Stoudenmire was sick [drunk?] and confined to bed unable to work.[8] He was able to resume his duties a week later. During his absence from duty he sent a letter to General King of the Texas Rangers. In this letter he upbraided the Ranger force, "I have always found them more ready to aggravate than to preserve the public peace, as well as taking sides with the lawless rather than the law abiding portion of town. . . The town is not in the state of quiet that I would like, and am satisfied that if any trouble should come up I would have more serious trouble if they were here than if they were absent."

General King immediately wrote to Capt. Baylor who then responded in a letter to King, " I can assure you that either he [Stoudenmire] used the long bow in his attack on the rangers or my memory is sadly at fault. I take it for granted that he was either drunk or under the influence of opium."[9] A month later Baylor moved his company back to Ysleta.

Within days of Stoudenmire's return to duty W. W. Mills made an attempt to unseat him. It was Mills' contention that the "city marshal has vacated his office by accepting an appointment as a Deputy United States Marshal."[10] Marshal Sherman of Santa Fe, New Mexico later confirmed this appointment. The *Lone Star* added it's voice to the conflict noting that Stoudenmire was negligent in turning over to the city the fines that he had been collecting.[11]

Mayor Joseph Magoffin, who had been elected in August, did his utmost to quell the mounting problems. He met with Stoudenmire to straighten out the accounts relating to fines. He checked on the validity of Mills' charges. At the next council meeting a unanimous vote declared the office of city marshal vacant. W. W. Mills was nominated for the vacant position by Alderman Hague. Stoudenmire was nominated by Alderman Schuster. Mayor Magoffin ended by breaking a tie vote and returning Stoudenmire to office maintaining the status quo. The reason behind this seemingly strange outcome was undoubtedly due to a combination of factional politics and a truce that was all but completed. Leaders in the community had been negotiating with both Stoudenmire and the Mannings. Two days later, April 16th, the truce was signed hopefully putting an end to the volatile feud. It read as follows:[12]

We the undersigned parties, having this day mutually settled all difficulties and unfriendly feelings existing between us, hereby agree that we will meet and pass each other on peaceable terms and that bygones shall be bygones, and that we will never allude in the future to any past animosities that have existed between us.

Signed

Dallas Stoudenmire

J. Manning

G. F. Manning

Frank Manning

Though Stoudenmire evidently avoided the Mannings the truce apparently had no effect on his drinking habits. He confronted W. W. Mills at the old Central Hotel and attempted to goad him into a gunfight. Mills wisely declined the gun that Dallas generously offered to loan him. He threatened to run the editor of the El Paso *Times* out of town. He threatened to shoot Alderman Phillips on sight, and he had a run-in with former Ranger Beaumont. The fact that he fell asleep dead drunk on a saloon floor stopped a gunfight from taking place.[13]

Finally realizing the hopelessness of the situation the city council met on May 27th. In a state of desperation they planned to ask for Stoudenmire's resignation. When they had gathered in the council chamber, in walked an inebriated Stoudenmire. Flashing his guns he proceeded to threaten those present, "I can straddle every God-damn alderman in this council."

James Manning (seated) and his wife, Leonor in about 1883.
Frank Manning is standing at the rear. (Courtesy of Leon Metz.)

A thoroughly shaken Mayor Magoffin adjourned the meeting before it had been called to order. Even his political allies now abandoned the beleaguered marshal.

When the council met two days later, it accepted Stoudenmire's letter of resignation:[14]

> Believing as I do that under the present administration of the city government my usefulness as city marshal will become materially impaired and learning that there will be an attempt to reduce the pay of the marshal, already too low, I hereby tender my resignation as city marshal. Before parting company with the officers of the city, while I feel that I have suffered an injustice from certain members of your honorable body, I think it is my duty to, and do hereby, apologize for my conduct in the council chamber last Saturday evening and beg to assure you that I meant no disrespect to your body or the people whom you represent.
>
> Dallas Stoudenmire

Jim Gillett was promptly nominated for city marshal by Alderman Schuster and was elected. Stoudenmire continued to reside in El Paso, and on July 13, managed to get an appointment as a Deputy United States Marshal for the western district of Texas. Two weeks later he got into a quarrel with one of his former assistants, William Page. He got off a shot, but Page deflected his aim. Bloodshed was diverted when Marshal Gillett covered the combatants with a double-barrel shotgun. Both were arrested and fined, and in addition, Dallas was placed under bond.[15]

Duties as a U. S. Marshal required Stoudenmire to make frequent trips up to New Mexico. One such trip to Deming raised the curtain on his final act.

The evening of September 17 he returned to El Paso on a train that arrived at about midnight. In his usual inebriated state he headed for the Acme saloon. It was his favorite watering hole, owned and operated by old friends originally from Columbus, Texas. Noting his condition, the bartender, C. C. Brooks, suggested he go home to bed. Stoudenmire objected, asking Brooks to close shop and visit some of the houses with him. When Brooks declined Dallas left the Acme and headed for Mannings saloon. He peered inside, turned around, and headed back to the Acme. By that time Brooks was getting set to close. An excited Tom Ochoa came in and began talking about someone making threats. Brooks got Ochoa to depart before Stoudenmire said anything. Brooks closed up the Acme and decided to humor Stoudenmire by accompanying him to Abbie Bell's place. Dallas called for his favorite gal Carrie who wasn't there at the moment. The madam said she was uptown eating but would soon return. Brooks parted company with Stoudenmire at 3 A. M. when Dallas entered Abbie Bell's to wait for Carrie.[16]

Almost the first person that Marshal Gillett ran into while making his early morning rounds was Dallas Stoudenmire. According to Jim, he was walking right down the middle of El Paso street, and it was obvious he had been on a spree. When Gillett offered to see him home the big man flared up saying he needed no assistance. Gillett turned and walked away. "I saw that just one imprudent word would bring on a difficulty. I did not wish to kill Stoudenmire even if I could, and at the same time I did not want to be killed by him." Stoudenmire then went home to bed.[17]

Later that morning the Mannings were informed that Stoudenmire had been on the prowl the previous night and had stopped by Frank's saloon looking for them. The fact that Dallas had apparently broken his solemn agreement enraged the Mannings. Jim immediately armed himself and headed for the Acme, threatening to have it out with Stoudenmire. Once there he had to content himself with haranging the bartender and saloon owners because Dallas was at home asleep.

Early in the afternoon Stoudenmire returned to the Acme. His friends, Neal Nuland, Cliff Brooks, and Walt Jones reproached him for hunting the Mannings at their saloon. Stoudenmire denied that he had been looking for trouble and claimed he had only been seeking someone for whom he had a warrant. Moodily he took a seat at the rear of the saloon.

Soon Frank Manning walked in and ordered a drink from Brooks. "I am damn sorry to see this thing happen," offered the bartender. "It is not my fault, I have tried every way to keep this thing down," responded Frank. Brooks made it known that he did not want trouble in his saloon to which Frank replied,

Dr. George Felix Manning with his family. Left to right: Tom, George Felix, Frank, Julia, and Sarah (Mrs. Manning). This photograph was taken in approximately 1890. (Courtesy of Leon Metz.)

"The sooner it comes off, the better for all parties." Stoudenmire passed them and stepped outside the saloon for a moment, and then returned to his seat. Neither party acknowledged the other's presence. Frank continued his conversation with Brooks, "I am the last man in the world to raise any disturbance. I am not going to bother anybody if they will leave me alone." Dr. Felix Manning came in next and joined Frank at the bar. Stoudenmire got up and left. Once again no acknowledgements were made. Tension was building.

Dallas strolled down San Antonio street to El Paso street, turned left, passed the Manning saloon, and entered the Gem saloon. He burst through the swinging door singing a song. He approached Al Nichols, a druggist, who was standing at the bar. "Them [the Mannings] sons of bitches have put up a job to kill me this evening," he said. Nichols advised him to go home, but Stoudenmire laughed and headed for the Pony Saloon.[18] Enroute he was informed that a warrant was being prepared for his arrest. Dallas made light of it indicating he would get Judge Blacker to straighten things out. Walt Jones, a former deputy and part owner of the Acme, then arrived on the scene. Stoudenmire asked him to explain to the Mannings that he wasn't hunting them the previous night, and added, "I want no trouble, but if they are bound to fight, I will fight any one of them."

Jones and Brooks tried to mediate the problem as the day wore on. They made a number of peace missions between the antagonists. The efforts appeared to be succeeding when a meeting was agreed upon. At 5:30 Jones accompanied Stoudenmire to Frank Manning's saloon with the avowed purpose of burying the hatchet with a handshake and drink. Jim Manning was standing at the bar and Dr. Manning was shooting billiards. Dallas called for Doc to join them at the bar for a drink. He then asked Jim where Frank was. "I don't know, but I'll go see if I can find him," said Jim as he left in search of his brother.

Dallas addressed Dr. Manning, "Some liars or damn S. O. B.'s have been trying to make trouble." The doctor replied "Dallas, you haven't stuck to the terms of your agreement." "Whoever says I have not tells a damned lie," fumed Stoudenmire. In a flash both men reached for their pistols. Walt Jones in a futile but courageous effort tried to jump between them. His actions only succeeded in throwing his friend Stoudenmire off balance. Dr. Manning drew faster and his first shot ripped into Dallas' left arm and chest causing him to drop his pistol. Manning's second shot hit a wallet and papers in Stoudenmire's right breast pocket jarring the big man thru the front door.[19]

Doctor Manning rushed out after his wounded opponent who at last returned a shot from his sawed off pocket pistol. It hit the doctor in his right elbow ending his career as a surgeon. Doc's pistol was sent flying. In sheer desperation, the little man rushed his much larger armed adversary pelting him in the face with his hat.[20] He then grabbed Stoudenmire and began wrestling to survive. In this scuffle the Doctor pinned Stoudenmire's arms down alongside his body so he could not bring his pistol into action. At that instant Jim Manning, having heard gunfire, came running up. He drew a sawed-off, triggerless .45 and fired. His first shot went wild splintering a nearby barber pole. His second shot, made at a closer range, hit Stoudenmire in the left temple killing him instantly. The two primary combatants tumbled into a heap on the street. Dr. Manning grabbed Stoudenmire's gun and began beating on the dead man's head. He was forcibly restrained and was lifted to his knees before he was convinced the danger was over and would release the gun. He promptly fainted from loss of blood.

The gunfire had also brought Marshal Gillett and Rangers Scott and Deaver on the run. They encountered dozens of men running away from the flying bullets, and were almost knocked off their feet several times. They arrived too late to intercede. Gillett informed Jim Manning that he and his brother were under arrest. Jim said, "All right marshal, but please help me carry my brother inside to bed. I think he is killed." The lawmen helped Jim carry his brother to his room in the back of the Manning saloon where Dr. Manning and his family lived.[21] Ranger Jim Deaver was placed on guard that evening to watch Jim and Doc in the family quarters.

A number of witnesses gave complete testimony at the inquest. The verdict reached was that, "Dallas Stoudenmire, on the evening of September 18, 1882, came to his death from a shot fired by a six-shooter .44 or .45 caliber in the hands of party unknown." This may well reflect uncertainty over which of the brothers fired the fatal shot. Judge Buckler's letter to Abe Campbell on September 19 seems to bear this out. "There were

Doc Manning at Flagstaff, Arizona, in about 1920. (Courtesy of Leon Metz.)

two of the Manning boys engaged in the difficulty, but it is not certain which one did the killing which was justifiable."

After further consideration the District Attorney prepared two indictments. Doctor Felix Manning was indicted for assault with intent to murder. Jim Manning was indicted for murder. In late October, both of the Mannings were acquited in separate trials. "There was no fundamental ground for conviction against Jim Manning" according to one-time District Attorney, W. W. Bridgers, who witnessed the events. "Seeing that Dr. Manning was unarmed and striving to protect himself against the armed Stoudenmire, Jim Manning was within his fundamental rights as a citizen in preventing Stoudenmire from killing the doctor—even to the point of killing Stoudenmire to stop him."[22]

In less than a year and a half after the big gunfight of April 14, 1881, Dallas Stoudenmire died on El Paso Street. His body lay in the dust only a few yards from the spot where George Campbell had fallen.

NOTES

1. *El Paso Times*, June 17, 1940.

2. *El Paso Herald*, November 20, 1909. Ranger abstract rolls, *Baylor Co. A* June-August 1881, Archives, Texas State Library, Austin; Leon C. Metz, *Dallas Stoudenmire*, p. 64.

3. Mrs. Lois Manning (widow of Dr. Manning's son) interview with Leon C. Metz, Tucson Feb. 16, 1966.

4. *El Paso Lone Star*, December 17, 1881; El Paso court records check by Bob McNellis.

5. Habeas Corpus documents covering slaying of Samuel M. "Doc" Cummings in possession of Leon C. Metz. Extensively quoted in Leon C. Metz, *Dallas Stoudenmire*, pp. 86-90; William Gilson interview with FRE, El Paso, 1981.

6. *Frontier Times*, Vol. 1, No. 10 (July 1924), p. 25.

7. Conrey Bryson, *The Land Where We Live*. El Paso: Anniversario Del Paso, 1973, p. 42.

8. El Paso City Council Minutes, Book C., Part 1, p. 46.

9. Stoudenmire to King, March 29, 1882. Baylor to King, April 26, 1882. Adjutant General's Office records, Austin.

10. El Paso City Council Minutes, Book C., Part 1, p. 61.

11. El Paso *Lone Star*, April 8, 1882.

12. El Paso City Council Minutes, Book C., p. 63-64; *Frontier Times* Vol. 1, No. 10 (July 1924), pp. 25-26; *El Paso Herald*, Sept. 20, 1882.

13. Mills, *Forty Years in El Paso*, p. 162, 164; *El Paso Herald* May 11, 1905; November 20, 1909.

14. El Paso City Council Minutes Book C., p. 72; *El Paso Herald*, May 11, 1905.

15. Gillett, *Six Years with the Texas Rangers*, p. 237.

16. *El Paso Herald*, September 20, 1882.

17. *Frontier Times*, Vol. 1, No. 10 (July 1924), p. 26.

18. Metz, *Dallas Stoudenmire*, pp. 115, 116.

19. Metz, *Dallas Stoudenmire*, p. 117, *Colorado County Citizen*, Sept. 28, 1882.

20. Sonnichsen, *Pass of the North*, Vol. 1, p. 245.

21. *Frontier Times*, Vol. 1, No. 10, p. 27.

22. Cunningham, *Triggernometry*, pp. 187,188.

The west side of El Paso Street as seen from the north. The wagon unloading barrels at the Manning Saloon stands just beyond the location where Stoudenmire was killed September 18, 1882. The barber pole by the leafy tree was one hit by Jim Manning's wild shot. The April 14, 1882, gunfight took place near the utility pole beyond the wagon. (Photo courtesy of Millard G. McKinney.)

Bibliography

BOOKS

Braun, Matthew *El Paso*. New York: Fawcett/Gold Medal, 1973. 239 pp.

Bryson, Conrey *The Land Where We Live*. El Paso: Guyness, 1973. 99 pp.

Calleros, Cleofas *El Paso Then and Now*. El Paso: American Printing Co., 1954. 224 pp.

Casey, Robert J. *The Texas Border*. New York: Bobbs-Merrill, 1950. 440 pp.

Cunningham, Eugene *Triggernometry*. Idaho: Caxton, 1941. 441 pp.

Douthitt, Katherine *Romance and Dim Trails*. Dallas: William T. Tardy Co., 1938. 280 pp.

Drago, Henry Sinclair *The Legend Makers*. New York: Dodd, Mead & Co., 1975. 239 pp.

Gillett, James B. *Six Years with the Texas Rangers*. New Haven, Connecticut: 1925. 332 pp.

Haley, J. Evetts *Charles Goodnight*. New York: Houghton-Mifflin, 1936. 485 pp.

Hunter, J. Marvin *The Trail Drivers of Texas.* Tennessee: Cokesbury, 1925. 1044 pp.

Jones, Harriet Howze *El Paso, A Centennial Portrait.* El Paso: El Paso County Historical Society, 1973. 292 pp.

Kohlberg, Ernst *Letters of Ernst Kohlberg.* El Paso: Texas Western Press, 1973. 71 pp.

Mangan, Frank *Bordertown Revisited.* El Paso: Guyness, 1973. 160 pp.

Mangan, Frank *El Paso in Pictures.* El Paso: The Press, 1971. 174 pp.

Metz, Leon C. *City at the Pass.* Woodland, California: Windsor, 1980. 126 pp.

Metz, Leon C. *John Selman.* New York: Hasting House, 1966. 254 pp.

Metz, Leon C. *The Shooters.* El Paso: Mangan Books, 1976. 300 pp.

Metz, Leon C. *Dallas Stoudenmire,* Austin, Texas: Pemberton Press, 1969. 162 pp.

Mills, W. W. *Forty Years at El Paso.* El Paso: Hertzog, 1962. 212 pp.

O'Neal, Bill *Encyclopedia of Western Gun Fighters.* Norman, Oklahoma: University of Oklahoma Press, 1979. 386 pp.

Orton, Brig. Gen. R. H. *Record of California Men, War of Rebellion.* California: California State Printing Office, 1890. 887 pp.

Pritchard, A. M. *Mead Relations.* Staunton, Virginia: McClure & Co., 1933. 265 pp.

Raine, William MacLeod *Famous Sheriffs & Western Outlaws.* New York: Doubleday & Doran, 1929. 294 pp.

Rosa, Joseph *The Gunfighter, Man or Myth.* Norman, Oklahoma: University of Oklahoma Press, 1969. 229 pp.

Siringo, Charles A. *A Texas Cowboy.* Nebraska: University of Nebraska Press, 1976. 316 pp.

Sonnichsen, C. L. *The El Paso Salt War.* El Paso: Texas Western, 1961. 75 pp.

Sonnichsen, C. L. *Pass of the North.* El Paso: Texas Western, 1968. 467 pp.

Sonnichsen, C. L. *I'll Die Before I'll Run.* Connecticut: Devin-Adair, 1961. 384 pp.

Stanley, F. *The San Marcial Story.* N.P., 1960. 18 pp.

Taylor, William C. *A History of Clay County.* Austin: Jenkins, 1974. 168 pp.

Webb, Walter Prescott *The Texas Rangers.* Austin: University of Texas, 1977. 583 pp.

Webb, Walter Prescott *The Handbook of Texas.* Austin: Texas State Historical Association, 1952. 977 pp.

White, Owen P. *Out of the Desert.* El Paso: McMath Co., 1923. 442 pp.

White, Owen P. *Texas, An Informal Biography.* New York: G. P. Putnam's Sons, 1945. 268 pp.

White, Owen P. *Them Was the Days.* New York: Minton, Balch & Co., 1925. 235 pp.

White, Owen P. *Trigger Fingers.* New York: G. P. Putnam's Sons, 1926. 323 pp.

MANUSCRIPTS AND LETTERS

Campbell Family Scrap Book, Wilmette, Illinois. George W. Campbell letters: A. J. Buckler letter to A. Campbell, Buckler Telegram, Judge Plemons letter to A. Campbell, O'Neil letter to Judge Plemons.

Capt. Baylor letter to Gen. King. September 20, 1881, Adj. Gen. office records, Barker Texas Historical Center, University of Texas, Austin.

George Look, "Reminiscences of June 13, 1909." El Paso Public Library, El Paso, Texas.

Judge Frank H. Douthitt letter to F.R. E., February 20, 1981.

Las Vegas New Mexico, 1880 Census, New Mexico State Archives.

El Paso City Council Minute Books.

Microfilm "Dispatches from U.S. Consul Juarez." Library, University of Texas, El Paso, Texas.

MAGAZINES

Frontier Times, July 1924. M. Hunter Publishing.

Guns of the Gunfighters, 1975. Peterson Publishing.

NEWSPAPERS

Ashland (Kentucky) *Independent*, May 1881.

Chicago Daily News, April 15, 1881.

Chicago Evening Journal, April 19, 1881.

Chicago Tribune, Jan. 12, 1880; Jan. 29, 1880; April 16 & 18, 1881.

Daily Interocean, April 18, 1881.

El Paso Evening Post, May 30, 1928.

El Paso Herald, Nov. 22, 1881; Dec. 28, 1881; Nov. 13 & 27, 1909.

El Paso Times, April 2, 1881; Jan. 1, 1882; June 25, 1916.

Galveston News, Jan. 28, 1880, Feb. 19, 1881.

Henrietta Shield, April, 1881.

Kansas City Evening Star, April 15, 1881.

Newman's Semi-Weekly, April 20, 1881.

Santa Fe, N.M., April 17, 1881.

Appendix

EL PASO CITY COUNCIL

Elected July 20, 1880
    Solomon Schutz   Mayor
    B. S. Dowell   First Ward Alderman
    (J.P. Hague evidently replaced Dowell upon Dowell's death in November 1880)
    Adolf Krakauer   First Ward Alderman
    J. D. Ochoa   Second Ward Alderman
    Antonio Hart   Second Ward Alderman
    S. C. Slade   Third Ward Alderman and City Clerk.
    Joseph Magoffin   Third Ward Alderman and mayor pro tem.

Joseph Magoffin was elected Mayor at the next election on August 9, 1881. Solomon Schutz was never again a member of the City Council.

James Price Hague was considered one of the leading lawyers of El Paso County by most judges and lawyers. *The Legal Heritage of El Paso*, (Texas Western Press, 1963).

Adolf Krakauer was born in Bavaria and came to El Paso in 1875. It is noted that he did bookkeeping for the Schutz Brothers store. He served as City Treasurer (Nov. 2, 1881, El Paso *Herald*), and opened a hardware store in 1885. He was elected mayor in a controversial election in 1889. He proved to be inelligible for office because he was not a U. S. Citizen.

J. D. Ochoa may have been a close relative of Don Ynocente Ochoa. The El Paso *Herald* (Dec. 28, 1881) notes that "Joe Bauer was fined $25 by Mayor Ochoa" during the week of May 18-25, 1881. This could refer to Don Ynocente in Paso del Norte. In El Paso, Texas, Mayor Schutz was back east on a 7 week trip. If Magoffin was also out of town, J. D. Ochoa may well have been filling in as acting mayor.

S. C. Slade was also serving as customs collector.

Dallas Stoudenmire became City Marshal on April 11, 1881, and he resigned on April 13, 1882.

LOCATIONS

In 1881 the City Hall was located in the old Hornic Building (adobe) at the intersection of Chuhuahua Street and San Francisco Street. A new city hall was erected at the Southwest corner of Overland and Santa Fe Streets in 1882.

The Schutz and the Ochoa stores, were both on the North side of San Francisco Street between Pioneer Plaza and Chihuahua Street.

Ynocente Ochoa's home was in Paso del Norte (Juarez) on the south side of 16th of September Street in the 500 block. He was the wealthiest man in town. Benito Juarez is reported to have lived at Ochoa's house during his 1865-1866 visit.

BURIALS

John W. Hale was first buried at his ranch in Conutillo, but later his body was transferred to Concordia Cemetery in El Paso.

George Campbell was initially buried in El Paso, but within days the body was shipped back to Ashland, Kentucky, for reburial in the family plot.

Gus Krempkau is buried in the San Antonio City Cemetery *1.

Dallas Stoudenmire is buried in the cemetery at Alleytown, Texas.

GENERAL

No evidence has come to light to show that either Chris Peveler or Frank Stevenson were ever convicted of murdering the two mexican vaqueros.

At 5 P. M. on the day prior to the big shootout, April 14, 1881, just 80 miles north in Mesilla, New Mexico, Billy the Kid was sentenced to hang.

Leon Metz uncovered the fact that, "Prior to Jim Manning's death Stuart Lake offered to write his biography. Manning declined and suggested that Lake see Wyatt Earp."

One hundred years to the day, April 14, 1981, after the gunfight the sound of guns again echoed thru El Paso. This time it was an 18 gun salute at Ft. Bliss in honor of Gen. Omar Bradley who at that moment was being buried at Arlington National Cemetery. Gen. Bradley had spent his last years in El Paso and had lain in state there for several days prior to his burial.

April 14, 1981: one hundred years after the big shoot-out. The author and his wife, Sharon, are made honorary citizens of El Paso and receive a key to the city. Making the presentation is noted author, Leon Metz, (left) the Executive Assistant to the mayor. (Author's collection.)

Fred R. Egloff

Fred R. Egloff is a native of the Chicago area and is a graduate of Loyola University. He first became interested in the history of El Paso when he was stationed at Fort Bliss as an Army officer in the mid-1950's.

He has pursued Western history as an avocation while following his career in industrial sales. This interest has led him to an active involvement in historical societies, historic preservation, and museum design. During the 1978-80 period, he was sheriff (president) of the Chicago Corral of the Westerners. He has written numerous articles on history for a variety of publications.

Egloff's approach to historic research is very thorough and includes the employment of books, archives, interviews, photo analysis and on-the-spot investigation (by horse if necessary). Fred is a member of the Western History Association, and the Western Writers of America.